George McKendree Steele

Outline Study of Political Economy

George McKendree Steele

Outline Study of Political Economy

ISBN/EAN: 9783337079536

Printed in Europe, USA, Canada, Australia, Japan

Cover: Foto ©Suzi / pixelio.de

More available books at **www.hansebooks.com**

OF

POLITICAL ECONOMY.

BY

GEORGE M. STEELE, LL.D.,

PRINCIPAL OF THE WESLEYAN ACADEMY, WILBRAHAM, MASS.

NEW YORK:
CHAUTAUQUA PRESS.
C. L. S. C. DEPARTMENT
1886.

COPYRIGHT, 1885,
BY PHILLIPS & HUNT,
805 BROADWAY, NEW YORK.

The required books of the C. L. S. C. are recommended by a Council of six. It must, however, be understood that recommendation does not involve an approval by the Council, or by any member of it, of every principle or doctrine contained in the book recommended.

ELECTROTYPED AND PRINTED
BY RAND, AVERY, AND COMPANY,
BOSTON.

TO THE

Alumni of the Lawrence University of Wisconsin,

AND ESPECIALLY

TO THE GRADUATES OF THE YEARS 1874 TO 1879,

WHO, WITH THE AUTHOR,

PURSUED THE STUDY OF THE SCIENCE, THE RUDIMENTS OF
WHICH ARE HEREIN SET FORTH,

This Little Volume

IS AFFECTIONATELY INSCRIBED.

"Man, the molecule of society, is the subject of social science. . . . His greatest need is that of ASSOCIATION with his fellow-men." "Association depends upon INDIVIDUALITY. There can be no association without differences." — CAREY.

"The higher a living being stands in the order of nature, the greater the difference between its parts, and between each part and the whole organism. The lower the organism, the less the difference between the parts, and between each part and the whole." — GOETHE.

"For the body is not one member, but many." "Many members, yet but one body." "Those members of the body which seem to be more feeble are necessary." "And whether one member suffer, all the members suffer with it; or one member be honored, all the members rejoice with it." — PAUL.

PREFACE.

This volume is designed to meet the wants of younger students, and those who have not had long discipline in severer studies. The fault with many of our elementary books on Political Economy has been, that they are condensations, rather than simplifications, of the subject. In such a study as this, where the great value lies in the illustrations, it is not easy to present the principles briefly, and at the same time to exhibit clearly their practical application. Yet this has been the special aim here, while at the same time great care has been taken to preserve the scientific form. Whether the writer has succeeded in accomplishing his purpose, it is for the public to determine. It is hoped, however, that the increasingly large number of students in the home college, and the students in our academies and high schools, as well as the general reader, will find in this short treatise both an interesting and a valuable aid in the attainment of information on a subject always of universal importance, and never more so than at the present time.

It has been the purpose, on the numerous controverted points, to set forth clearly both sides of the subject, while there is no attempt to conceal the convictions of the writer.

The author has drawn largely upon the works of Henry C. Carey. In respect to the labor-question he is specially indebted to Professor Francis A. Walker's able treatises. The late Professor Jevons has furnished valuable aid on the Instrument of Exchange. Other writers are cited as occasion has demanded.

CONTENTS.

INTRODUCTORY CHAPTER.
DEFINITIONS AND PRELIMINARY STATEMENTS.

                                                              PAGE

1. Relation of Social Science to Political Economy.—2. Wealth.—3. Value: general notion.—4. Chief element of value; cost of production.—5. Capital as pre-existent labor an element in value. Exertion and abstinence.—6. Utility an essential characteristic of value. Definition. When more or less prominent.—7. Utility not the measure of value. Sometimes in an inverse ratio. Full definition of value.—8. Further consideration of wealth. Full statement of its import.—9. MAN the proper subject of Political Economy, not mere material wealth.—10. Economy, husbandry, not parsimony. *Political* Economy has reference to man in society. Association and individuality the great forces of civilized humanity.—11. General divisions of the subject . . .   1

BOOK FIRST.—PRODUCTION.

CHAPTER I.
PRODUCTIVE AGENCIES.

1. Production defined and illustrated. Two great agencies, nature and man. Man furnishes labor. Nature supplies (1) materials, (2) forces.—2. Labor defined; consists in *effecting changes*   9

CHAPTER II.

APPLICATION OF LABOR TO PRODUCTION.

1. Application of labor, direct and indirect. Direct labor of three kinds,— transformation, transmutation, and transportation. — 2. Indirect application: more obvious. Five kinds: 1. Preparation of material; 2. Manufacture of implements; 3. Providing sustenance; 4. Furnishing clothing, shelter, etc.; 5. Protecting the laborers. — 3. Among the less obvious forms of indirect labor are: 1. Organizing, superintending, etc.; 2. The rearing of children; 3. Education; 4. The professions; 5. Invention and discovery. — 4. Labor not the sole condition of wealth. Mind and character 14

CHAPTER III.

PRODUCTIVE AND UNPRODUCTIVE LABOR.

1 Disagreement among writers. — 2. Several kinds of effort generally allowed to be unproductive: 1. Misdirected labor; 2. That of which the ultimate object is destructive; 3. All purely speculative projects; 4. That which is expended in ministering to vicious appetites 20

CHAPTER IV.

CAPITAL.

1. Capital the fruit of abstinence, but not of abstinence alone. — 2. A capitalist not necessarily a rich man. Professor Bowen on the beginnings of capital. — 3. Relation of capital to wealth. — 4. Wealth which is not capital. — 5. Fixed and circulating capital. — 6. Capital must be consumed. — 7. Nearly all wealth the result of recent production. — 8. Change of circulating into fixed capital. — 9. Effect of the invention of labor-saving machinery 23

CHAPTER V.

RELATIONS OF CAPITAL AND LABOR.

1. Generally that of mutual dependence. — 2. Capital furnishes conditions of labor. Doctrine of the limitation of labor by

capital subject to a variety of modifications. Still true in general that a small amount of capital employs a small amount of labor.—**3**. Effect of unproductive expenditure of the rich on the welfare of the poor. 31

CHAPTER VI.

SOME CONDITIONS OF HIGHEST PRODUCTION.

1. Combination and division of labor. Association and individuality.—**2**. Combination of two kinds, simple and complex.—**3**. Diverse processes in a single trade. Vast increase of productive power thus effected.—**4**. Direct benefits of division of labor.—**5**. Limitations to division of labor.—**6**. Some disadvantages 34

CHAPTER VII.

CONDITIONS OF HIGHEST PRODUCTION, *continued*.

1. Diversification of industry. This diversification as far as possible in each community.—**2**. Diverse tastes and aptitudes to be met, otherwise much productive force lost.—**3**. Freedom of labor and commerce. This freedom to be real, and not merely theoretical. The largest liberty always under some restrictions.—**4**. General education, a great productive power.—**5**. Moral character an important condition 42

BOOK SECOND.—CONSUMPTION.

CHAPTER I.

NATURE AND VARIOUS FORMS OF CONSUMPTION.

1. Production implies consumption; that is, the destruction of values.—**2**. Re-appearance of the value destroyed, in other forms.—**3**. Voluntary or involuntary 49

CHAPTER II.

PRODUCTIVE AND UNPRODUCTIVE CONSUMPTION.

1. The difference not always easy to determine. — 2. Much obviously unproductive. — 3. Necessaries, conveniences, and luxuries 53

CHAPTER III.

PUBLIC CONSUMPTION.

1. The support of government. — 2. Principles which should control in public expenditure. — 3. Expenditure for general education. — 4. Pauperism. — 5. War and national defence . . 57

BOOK THIRD. — EXCHANGE.

CHAPTER I.

PRINCIPLES WHICH FORM THE BASIS OF EXCHANGE.

1. Definition and explanation. — 2. How related to association and individuality. — 3. Exchange between remote communities. — 4. "Commerce" and "Trade." Obstacles to direct exchange 65

CHAPTER II.

THE LAW OF EXCHANGE.

1. *Value for Value.* Reference to the nature of value. — 2. Conditions modifying the law. No general rise and fall of values. — 3. Supply and demand. Terms explained. The general principle as affecting value. — 4. Further limitation of these terms. — 5. How increase of supply by diminishing value increases demand. — 6. The principle modified in cases of limited production. — 7. The law still further modified by other circumstances 70

CHAPTER III.

THE PROMOTION OF COMMERCE.

1. Whatever tends to promote association aids commerce. — 2. Benefit of rapid and immediate exchange. — 3. Proximity of producer and consumer. Facilities of transportation. — 4. Variety of products 77

CHAPTER IV.

PROTECTION AND FREE TRADE.

1. Design of a protective tariff. Free trade. — 2. Arguments in favor of protection: 1. Defence against unequal competition of older and richer societies; 2. A steady and uniform market; 3. Tends to societary completeness; 4. Advantage to general interests other than those directly protected. Three advantages to agriculture; 5. Prevents degradation of labor 82

CHAPTER V.

ARGUMENTS IN FAVOR OF FREE TRADE.

1. Positive arguments: 1. Method of nature; 2. Conserves and increases the productive power of labor; 3. The right of property implies freedom of exchange; 4. All restriction on commerce between two nations injures the interests of both; 5. Freedom of commercial intercourse tends to peace and good-will between nations. — 2. Objections to the protective system: 1. Violates the right of every man to do what he will with his own; 2 Protective duties of the nature of a tax upon all other industries; 3. Diminishes exports; 4. Infant industries protected never come to maturity; 5. If good between nations, why not between different parts of the same nation, as in the United States? 6. Gives monopoly privileges. — 3. Comparative strength of arguments on both sides. Argument from fear of degradation of labor. — 4. Force of argument from success of free trade between parts of a large nation. — 5. Free trade as the "method of nature." — 6. Examination of the objection that protective duties are of the

nature of a tax. — **7.** Do protective duties cause diminution of exports? — **8.** Brief summary of results 90

CHAPTER VI.
THE INSTRUMENT OF EXCHANGE.

1. Money the means of enhancing the facility of association. — **2.** Original exchange by barter. Its inconveniences. Trade a partial remedy 103

CHAPTER VII.
THE PRECIOUS METALS.

1. Eight characteristics desirable in any substance used as a medium of exchange. These found to a considerable extent in gold and silver, though not all of them to the full extent sometimes claimed. — **2.** Why these metals are used for this purpose. Coinage. — **3.** Relation of government to money. Legal tender. — **4.** Monetary standard. — **5.** Relative value of gold and silver 105

CHAPTER VIII.
CERTAIN DOCTRINES CONCERNING MONEY EXAMINED.

1. Money not synonymous with wealth. — **2.** Value of money in circulation only a small fraction of that of the commodities exchanged. — **3.** Relation of the amount of money to general prices 112

CHAPTER IX.
THE CREDIT ELEMENT IN THE INSTRUMENT OF EXCHANGE.

1. Money only a minor proportion of the machinery of exchange. — **2.** Early suggestion of credit. Book account. Transfer of credit. — **3.** Definition of credit. — **4.** Advantages of credit: 1. To capitalists; 2. To non-capitalists.— **5.** What is loaned frequently, not money, but other capital reckoned as money 117

CHAPTER X.

BANKS AND BANKING.

1. Nature and history of banks. — 2. Origin of banks. Banks of deposit. — 3. Banks in relation to credit. — 4. Abridgment of the use of money by bank-checks and drafts. — 5. The clearing-house. — 6. How commodities pay for commodities through the facilities afforded to credit by means of banks. — 7. Four kinds, or functions, of banks. Savings banks described. Their advantages. — 8. Banks of discount and loan. — 9. Banks of issue or circulation. — 10. Banks deal not so much in money as in debits and credits. Small proportion of money used in large banking-transactions 122

CHAPTER XI.

PAPER CURRENCY OF THE UNITED STATES.

1. National-bank system. — 2. Government notes, or "greenbacks." — 3. Advantages and disadvantages of a paper currency 133

BOOK FOURTH. — DISTRIBUTION.

CHAPTER I.

GENERAL STATEMENT.

1. Definition and illustration. — 2. Difficulty of determining the just proportions of product to each producer. — 3. General division of subject: 1. Wages; 2. Profit; 3. Interest; 4. Rent; 5. Taxes 139

CHAPTER II.

WAGES: GENERAL VIEW.

1. Limitation of term. Wages, salary, fees, etc. — 2. Theory of a laboring-class. "Wages-fund." — 3. Objections to the phrase, "laboring-class." — 4. Minimum rate of wages . . . 144

CHAPTER III.

WAGES AS AFFECTED BY VARIOUS CIRCUMSTANCES.

PAGE

1. Nominal and real wages. — **2.** Conditions to be taken note of in estimating real value of wages. — **3.** Wages also affected by character of the labor. — **4.** Influence of the industrial system of a community as affecting wages 147

CHAPTER IV.

HIGH AND LOW WAGES AS RELATED TO DEAR AND CHEAP LABOR.

1. Labor dear or cheap according as there is a larger or smaller amount of product for a given amount of wages. — **2.** Theory of *necessary rate* of wages as affecting prospect of improvement in condition of laborers. E. P. Smith's views 150

CHAPTER V.

"THE WAGES-FUND."

1. If the theory is correct, no improvement for the laborer except in the restriction of the population. — **2.** Relation of wages to product. — **3.** F. A. Walker's views. Wages not paid out of capital, but out of product 153

CHAPTER VI.

CAREY'S LAW OF THE INCREASE OF WAGES.

1. As society advances, there is an increase of the laborers', and a decrease of the capitalists', *proportion* of the joint product of labor and capital; while there is to both an increased *amount*. — **2.** Illustration from the beginnings of capital with the savage. — **3.** Axe of stone, of bronze, of iron, of steel. — **4.** Corroborated by facts 156

CHAPTER VII.

REMEDIES FOR LOW WAGES.

1. Possibility of remedies. — **2.** Can Government do any thing? What it cannot and what it can do. — **3.** "Strikes." Good and evil of them. — **4.** "Trades-unions." Two objects of these. Economical and uneconomical measures. — **5.** *Co-operative association.* Its methods. — **6.** Difficulties in the way of it. Importance of the office of an *employer.* — **7.** *Copartnership of industry.* Its method and advantages. Harmony with principles previously laid down. — **8.** The wages of women 160

CHAPTER VIII.

PROFITS.

1. Portion of product going to the employer. The latter not necessarily a capitalist. — **2.** Economy of conceding to an employer a larger proportion of the product than to a common or even a skilled laborer. — **3.** The risk and uncertainty of business an element to be considered in calculating the claim of profits. Profits not in conflict with wages. — **4.** *Patent and copy rights.* Their significance and economy 170

CHAPTER IX.

INTEREST.

1. Extent of its signification. — **2.** Rate of interest, on what it depends: 1. Amount of money in circulation; 2. Profits of business; 3. Scarcity or uncertainty of capital; 4. Facility of re-conversion of evidences of debt. 174

CHAPTER X.

RENT.

1. Rent in this country as compared with the same in Europe. Relation to the value of land. — **2.** Importance of land. — **3.** What constitutes value in land? Doctrines of the British economists. II. C. Carey's views. — **4.** Ricardo's theory of rent. — **5.** Consequences of the theory. — **6.** Influences which retard the operations of the law. — **7.** The theory compared with facts of history. — **8.** The fallacy in the theory. The most productive soils not first occupied. — 9. True theory of value of land. The same as the value of other things. — 10. Rent or value of land affected by various minor considerations: 1. Fertility; 2. Facility of cultivation; 3. Situation 178

CHAPTER XI.

TAXATION.

1. Under the principle of division of labor, there must be some agency for the protection of the laborer. Government and its relation to production. — 2. Economy of taxation. — 3. Whether taxation should be according to property or revenue. — 4. Uniformity of taxation practically impossible and uneconomical. — 5. Direct and indirect taxation. — 6. Comparative merits of the two methods. — 7. Forms of direct taxation: 1. Income-tax; 2. Assessment of total property. Faults of any system yet devised. — 8. Other methods proposed. 188

POLITICAL ECONOMY.

INTRODUCTORY CHAPTER.

DEFINITIONS AND PRELIMINARY STATEMENTS.

1. SOCIAL SCIENCE treats of the natural laws which govern men in their relations to each other. Political economy is the application of that portion of these laws which pertain to the production and distribution of wealth.

2. It is important to understand what is meant by *wealth*. Writers differ greatly concerning its definition; but they all agree, by implication at least, in making *value* an essential characteristic of the objects symbolized by this term. It will, then, be necessary, before going on to a final determination of the signification of wealth, to ascertain the meaning of value.

3. As this is, in some respects, the most important word in political economy, it is desirable to get a clear apprehension of what it implies. Value is a *relative* term, having reference to the quantity of one commodity which may be equitably exchanged for a given quantity of another. Thus a bushel of wheat may be given for two bushels of oats, or a cord of wood for twenty yards of cotton cloth. But, in every instance of relationship, there must be some ground of the relation. The determination of this is essential to an adequate definition.

4. The chief element in the value of any thing, and that which constitutes its original standard, is the *cost of its production;* and by *cost*, we mean the *labor* involved. Labor may be defined as *the voluntary effort put forth by man to secure some desired object.* But when we say that value is estimated by the amount of labor necessary to produce an article, some care is required lest the statement mislead. It is not the amount of labor actually expended in the production which measures the value. A yard of cotton cloth made a hundred years ago involved the labor, perhaps, of several days; but its value, if now in the market, would be less than that of the same commodity of the present day, which involves the labor of not a tenth part as much time. It is, then, the labor which would be required to *reproduce* or replace an article, which determines its value.

5. But when we speak of labor as the principal ground of the relation which we denominate value, it is not labor in the form of immediate exertion alone that is meant. A large part of the labor which creates value is implied in the existence of tools and implements, and other contrivances. These constitute *capital*. This has sometimes been called "pre-existent labor." It will be sufficient for our present purpose to define it as *the result of previous labor, employed in further production.*

The design of all labor is to secure objects for the gratification of desire. Now, this gratification may be immediate, or it may be postponed for the sake of some greater gratification. In other words, the objects secured by labor may be consumed at once, or they may be wholly or partly reserved for use in securing other objects. All that is thus reserved is of the nature of capital. It is the result of labor; but the point to be observed is, that its existence is due, not to labor alone, but to *abstinence* as well. We thus arrive at a modified form of our statement concerning value; namely, that it is estimated by the amount of *sacrifice* involved in the production of a commodity; and that this sacrifice is of two kinds, — *exertion* and *abstinence*.

6. But there is another essential characteristic of value, which involves a further modification of our definition; this is *utility*. It has sometimes been confounded with value, and some writers speak of it as *value in use*. But it is clearly a distinct element. It may be defined as comprising *all those qualities in objects which make them desirable*. It will be readily seen that there are some things which have the greatest utility, and at the same time have little or no value: they are such objects as cost nothing; that is, such as involve no labor in their production. Thus air and sunshine, and, to a great extent, water, ordinarily cost nothing; and yet they are of the highest utility. It is often the case, that the utility of articles is almost inversely as their value. Iron is of very small *value* as compared with gold, and gold is of equally small *utility* as compared with iron. That utility is essential to value, is evident from the fact that no one would make any sacrifice for an object which would gratify no desire. Yet the prominence of this element in the determination of value varies widely: sometimes it is paramount, at other times its influence is so feeble as to be scarcely perceptible. When a man buys a barrel of flour, he expects, under ordinary circumstances, to pay a price somewhere nearly corresponding to the cost of its production. The utility, though maintaining an essential influence, is not palpably considered. But suppose some extraordinary conditions, by means of which there is not more than flour enough in the market to supply one-third of the demand, and that no more can be had for several weeks, or perhaps months. Those who have plenty of means will offer prices which are far out of proportion to the cost of production, and which will be measured almost wholly by the intensity of desire for the article. A man of means will pay several times the natural value of the commodity, rather than let his family suffer. It is obvious, that, in such a case, *utility*, and not *labor*, becomes the paramount element in the determination of value.

7. But it is, after all, doubtful if utility is a radical element in the measurement of value. It unquestionably has much to do in its temporary modification, through various disturbing influences operating upon the market. But it can hardly be regarded as in any proper sense a standard by which to estimate value.

Value and utility are often found in the inverse ratio of each other; that is, as value increases, utility diminishes, and *vice versa*. But it is not correct to say that this is *always* the case. If it were, infinitude of value would imply zero of utility. But, as we have seen, an object destitute of utility can have no value. Mr. Carey's description of the two is, that "the utility of things is the measure of man's power over nature;" while value is "the measure of nature's power over man," or of "the resistance which nature makes to man." These statements, while not altogether adequate as definitions, imply profound philosophical truths.

This, then, I would present as a proper and final definition of value: *Man's estimate of the amount of sacrifice requisite to the attainment of a desired object.*

8. We may now return to the subject of *wealth*. If we regard wealth as comprising all things that have value, we shall not be far out of the way. But at this point we meet a conflict of opinions among economists. Many, and perhaps a majority, of writers limit the term to *material* things. They make no account, in this respect, of those mental and moral acquisitions which constitute so large a proportion of the means of enjoyment and prosperity to humanity. The maker of a violin is in possession of an article which is to him a portion of wealth. But the skill and talent of Paganini, or Ole Bull, or any inferior musician who can so use the instrument as to gratify the popular taste, are not, on that account, reckoned by these writers as of any value in an economical sense; nor do these abilities constitute any part of the wealth of the community. Yet without this competence residing in some person, the violin could have no value. The same may be said concerning the abilities of various other classes who have acquired power to minister to the gratification of human desires. These are conditioned on labor, just as any kind of wealth is; and their utilities are not only just as real as those of material objects, but they are vastly more extensive. Without them, there would be no wealth worthy the name.

These considerations lead to the following definition: *Wealth comprises all those useful things and qualities, the attainment of which involves sacrifice on the part of man.* As value implies a certain degree of resistance to man on the part of nature, so wealth implies in man a certain degree of power over nature. Hence Mr. Carey's statement, that wealth is "the power to command the always gratuitous services of nature." When man is at his weakest, socially or individually, nature does nothing for him. Every infant, if dependent on nature alone, would inevitably perish. In the infancy of society, it is only by the most strenuous exertion that a precarious subsistence is secured. But, with every increment of power in man, nature multiplies her services.

They are not bought, but freely given, and given as soon as man is able to command them. In the most advanced civilization, the forces of nature have become so subservient to man, that, in thousands of cases, one can accomplish what a score, or sometimes even a hundred, could not formerly have done. It is this increase of power, more than that of material commodities, which constitutes the real wealth of the world.

9. It is easy to see, from what has already been said, that the proper subject of political economy is *man*. The laws pertaining to the underlying science are found in the character of man, — his tastes, his desires, the motives influencing him, and the limitations to which he is subject. The results arrived at are, his happiness and prosperity, his freedom, and his mastery over nature. This view differs from that entertained by many writers. With them it is regarded as the science of material wealth, and man is treated only as an important incident. Yet social science, of which political economy is an art, if it exist at all, is a science of man, and not of his accidents or appurtenances.

10. The word *economy* is from a Greek compound, and is nearly equivalent to our Saxon word *husbandry*. It has reference to the prudent management, by a householder, of his means, so as to secure the largest possible advantage for himself and his family. It is hardly necessary to remark, that economy is not the same as parsimony or frugality. It does not consist in mere abstinence for the sake of saving. It is rather a wise use of means and forces, so as to make them productive of the largest desired results.

Political economy, as the name implies, has reference to man in society, and not as an individual. One of man's greatest needs — perhaps his very greatest — is that of *association*. The solitary individual is only a minute constituent of man, in man's relation to the great purposes of life. Separated from his fellows, he would be, even in his individual capacity, but a small fraction of what he is when associated with them. No man is complete in himself. Each individual must be supplemented by others, generally by many others, and find a large part of his own competence in this association. Each has something that another lacks, and we are made to be sources of mutual supply to our several wants.

But not only is association essential to man, but *individuality* is equally essential. A superficial thinker might regard these two characteristics as antagonistic. The fact is so far otherwise, that each of them is actually dependent on the other. No man would associate with another unless the one had something which the other wanted. But for this, there would be no commerce. Two hatters making the same kind of hats would neither of them have any thing which the other would want. Men of the same mental habits and requirements could not benefit one another. Men must *differ*, or they will not associate; and the greater the difference, the greater the association.

On the other hand, it is only by association that the individual advances, and the highest development takes place. By such advancement and development, and by such only, the differences among men become great and numerous. In the lower grades of humanity, there is comparatively little difference between individuals; and there, too, the association is very slight. It is only in an advanced civilization that a strongly marked individuality exists, and that there are those numerous differences which make the mutual dependence the greatest.

11. Having given this brief general view of the subject, and defined some of its principal terms, we may now proceed with an examination of the principles involved in it. The subject is divided into four great branches, as follows: —

I. PRODUCTION, which treats of the creation of wealth.

II. CONSUMPTION, which treats of the destruction of wealth, and the laws which govern it.

III. EXCHANGE, which comprises the forms of commerce, or the transfer of commodities between different parties.

IV. DISTRIBUTION, which has reference to the apportionment of wealth among the parties who produce it.

BOOK FIRST.

PRODUCTION.

CHAPTER I.

PRODUCTIVE AGENCIES.

1. PRODUCTION consists in rendering the utilities of nature available to man. Some of these are furnished spontaneously, or without human effort. Others require only slight exertion. But generally, though the resources of nature are inexhaustible, and readily offer themselves under the proper conditions, these conditions must be furnished in the form of man's labor.

There are two great agencies which must co-operate in production, — *nature* and *man*. Man furnishes *labor*. This includes not only muscular exertion, but all the mental effort — the study, care, and anxiety — involved in securing objects of desire. Nature furnishes all the *material* upon which labor is to be exerted, and all the *forces* without which it would be ineffectual.

1. Nature supplies *materials*. In the simplest and most rudimentary style of human living, the desires of men are few, and easily satisfied. Fruits and nuts may be had for the gathering. Wild animals may furnish meat. There are caves and hollow trees which serve for shelter. Still some effort is requisite to secure the sustenance, and to render the shelter tenable. The animals must be hunted and slain, and their flesh prepared, although it be in the rudest manner. Fruits must be gathered, and the caves and cavities shaped

and in some way adapted. As society is developed, and as improvements are made, there will be additional desires prompting to additional exertions ; and the material to which these are to be applied will be forthcoming in the forms of wood, minerals, the skins of beasts and their coverings, the soils of the earth and those things which spring out of them. These comprise an almost endless variety of materials to which industry may be applied.

2. But nature furnishes not only materials, but also *forces*, to aid man in his productive efforts. The more obvious and palpable of these are gravitation, wind, explosive agencies; the expansive power of steam, magnetism, electricity, and the forces of vegetation. There are also numerous passive powers or properties of matter, which, when adopted by man, give him untold advantage. Such are the mechanical powers of the lever, inclined plane, and pulley, and those qualities of the metals which render them capable of taking an edge for cutting-purposes, as also malleability, ductility, and elasticity.

2. Labor has been defined as the voluntary effort put forth by man to secure objects of desire. We have seen that nature furnishes the material upon which labor is to be exerted, and the efficient forces through which production is effected. These materials and forces are supplied gratuitously. Nature is not parsimonious in this respect. The more we avail ourselves of her help, the more ready she is to help us ; and the greater the advantage we get over her, the more lavishly she bestows her gifts upon us.

Labor, then, consists not in creating things, but in *moving them;* that is, in *effecting changes*. It directs the natural forces to the service of man, and it is in this that production chiefly consists. It can move materials and objects into positions where these forces can act upon them with the desired effect. Thus an agricultural laborer can effect such changes in the soil as are requisite to the growth of corn, and he can place the seed in the ground; but he cannot make the crop. It is as impossible for him to create a kernel of grain as to make a planet. Labor may move fuel to the fire-place, and may properly dispose it for ignition; it may move a match, which by a previous motion has caught fire, to the prepared fuel: but the kindling flame, the heat and its effects in cooking food or transforming water into steam, are the results of energies and properties which man could never invent. It is nevertheless true, that, without the agency of labor by which the changes are made, none of these effects would follow. Nature does ten thousand things without the co-operation of man. She even furnishes innumerable utilities; but by herself she is not a producer, she creates no value.

CHAPTER II.

APPLICATION OF LABOR TO PRODUCTION.

1. THE application of labor to production is of two kinds, *direct* and *indirect*. The direct changes effected by labor may be embraced under the three heads of *transmutation, transformation,* and *transportation;* or, a change of elements, a change of form, and a change of place. They are also spoken of as chemical, mechanical, and commercial changes. The first finds its most common examples in agriculture. The seed is put in certain relations to the soil; and thus are furnished conditions of marvellous changes in the elements, drawn from both the earth and the atmosphere. But this kind of change is not limited to agriculture. It is exemplified in the rendering of ores, and the manufacture of soap, butter, cheese, etc.

Changes in form are seen in the mechanical arts. Leather is transformed into shoes, cloth into garments, and lumber into houses and cabinet-ware.

Changes in place are seen when a commodity is produced in one locality, and desired in another where it cannot be produced. Coal is found in the mountains of Pennsylvania, and carried to New York, Boston, and hundreds of other places where it is needed.

2. The *indirect* application of labor to production is of far more importance than is popularly attached to it. A little reflection will convince us that the direct effort put forth in effecting changes is only a small fraction of the whole labor involved. In indicating the several distinct forms of indirect labor, we may make a general division into *the more obvious* and *the less obvious*.

The more obvious.

1. In a large majority of instances, the material from which a commodity is to be produced by direct labor must be previously prepared. In the building of a house, a few carpenters, masons, and other artisans are employed. But the lumber, timber, bricks, stone, nails, paint, paper, etc., have to be furnished to these workmen by other producers; and the material out of which the latter prepare some of these has to be provided by laborers still back of them. Nature, it is true, furnishes all the original material; but it must often pass through several processes before it is fit for its final uses.

2. Another form of the indirect application of labor is seen in the manufacture of implements which the direct laborer uses. The farmer must have ploughs, cultivators, carts, etc.; each of the makers of these must also have tools to work with: and so on, back to the simplest forms of handicraft.

3. For the workers in any occupation, *sustenance* must be provided. Hence those who produce the food upon which the direct laborers subsist are indirectly helping in the creation of the value resulting.

4. Another form of indirect labor is the preparation of shelter, clothing, and fuel for the direct workers. Under this head, too, is to be reckoned the erection of buildings for any manufacturing or mechanical business. These are essential to every such enterprise, and the labor involved is to be considered in estimating the value of the final product.

5. *The protection of the laborers*, their implements, materials, and products, is also an item in the indirect application of labor. It is necessary to have agents selected by society, to guard against fraud, violence, and intimidation. They are a condition of profitable exertion, and their services are to be reckoned among the costs of all production.

3. *The less obvious* forms of indirect labor.

The foregoing comprise most of the more obvious forms of the indirect application of labor to production. There are other, not so conspicuous yet very important, ways in which labor more remotely, but still actually, contributes to this end. To some of these less obvious forms of indirect labor, I now call attention.

1. There is the work of organizing, superintending, and managing a business enterprise. Every one knows how much depends, even in small undertakings, on wise calculations, careful plans, and judicious oversight; and how, for want of these, there has often been a vast expenditure of labor to very little profit. Hence the organizers and managers of enterprises are to be reckoned as contributors to the product.

2. All the labor comprised in the raising of children, who are themselves to become laborers, is to be reckoned here. This demands the expenditure of much effort on the part of parents and others. Were their labor to be wanting, the productive force of the world would soon cease.

3. The labor involved in education is also clearly subsidiary to production. In this is embraced all that adds to the power and efficiency of the individual man. The labor may be that of the teacher or of the pupil, of instruction or of learning. Some of the most important vocations require no small amount of mental training in those who follow them. It is true, these are comparatively few: but all of the industries

require more or less intelligence; and the more of this any worker has, other things being equal, the greater will be his productive efficiency. Certainly there is no calling in which ignorance is an advantage: an idiot would not do for even a hod-carrier.

4. In the class of indirectly productive labor is comprised that of the so-called *professions*. Physicians, by their knowledge and skill, preserve the health which would otherwise become impaired, or restore that already impaired, and thus furnish laboring ability to the community, which would not exist but for their agency. The lawyer puts forth productive power in another way: if a laborer has a legal question which it would require days, and perhaps weeks, for him to investigate and determine, but which a lawyer who has prepared himself by previous discipline and experience can determine in a few hours, at a cost to the laborer of only a quarter of the labor which he might have otherwise vainly spent, is there not here a clear and undeniable gain to the productive force of the community?

The clergyman furnishes none of the commodities which are commonly reckoned as constituting wealth; but if, through his ministries, diligence, temperance, frugality, and integrity are promoted, and indolence, sensuality, and dishonesty are diminished, he certainly furnishes conditions of a larger productiveness than would otherwise exist; and thus his labor is, in a marked though indirect way, applied to production.

5. Into this category come also *inventors* and *discoverers*. Among the latter we include the men of science, who, by their investigations, bring to light new forces and agencies, or new combinations of those which nature furnishes in aid of human labor. The former are those whose skill enables them to apply these in the various devices and contrivances

which constitute the efficiency of machinery. The marvellously multiplied resources accruing to humanity by these means are familiar to the most ordinary intelligence.

These are some of the chief ways in which human exertion, though not very obviously related to production, does not the less actually enhance it to a manifold extent. There are also others, which there is no need to enumerate.

4. It is perhaps worth our while, at this point, to notice an error to which many of our recent economists have given encouragement. We have been taught that wealth is the creation of labor alone. The impression is made, whether intentional or not, that this labor is solely physical exertion. Demagogues have seized upon this notion, and have instilled into the minds of uneducated workingmen that the latter have created all the wealth comprised in massive buildings, in bridges and aqueducts, in great ships and ocean steamers, in railroads and canals, in complicated machinery and costly wares. This doctrine would be safe enough if it were true. But it is not true, and is therefore unwholesome and pernicious. Certainly the things spoken of could not have existed without physical toil; but, just as certainly, physical toil alone could never have produced more than an insignificant fraction of them. Of incalculably greater importance have been the mental qualities called into requisition. It is also further to be considered, — and the consideration is more important than any yet named, — that *character* is, after all, the most potent condition of wealth. A great part of the error to which I here allude consists in putting the ethical aspects of the question out of sight. But these cannot be ignored without vitiating the whole discussion. Upon the moral character of a society, more than upon all other things, depends its productive and especially its accumulative power. No qualities are so essential to the existence of wealth as industry, frugality, and self-denial. There will be little wealth in a community where fraud, injustice, and sensuality are the ruling characteristics. This makes an important proposition, previously announced, more evident; namely, that *man* is the proper subject of political economy.

CHAPTER III.

PRODUCTIVE AND UNPRODUCTIVE LABOR.

1. THERE is no very general agreement as to what constitutes the difference between productive and unproductive labor. Some deny that there is any such thing as unproductive labor: others restrict productive labor to that which results in material wealth. According to the latter, Daniel Webster, Horace Greeley, and Professor Agassiz were not producers, but the men who made their shoes and furnished their provisions were. Still other writers enlarge the sphere of productive laborers by reckoning as such all who indirectly contribute to production.

If we accept the definitions previously given of labor, production, and value; and if we admit, even without accepting it as a definition, that "wealth is the power which man has to command the gratuitous services of nature," — then we shall be obliged to admit, that not only all the various classes of laborers to which reference is made in the last chapter, but that all who labor in any art the design of which is to gratify any legitimate desire of man, are productive laborers. For, this capability of gratifying desire is an essential condition of wealth; and when furnished by any kind of effort, whether the product takes on a permanent form awaiting future consumption, or is consumed at the instant of production, it is all the same; for nothing can be regarded as a product which is not destined to be, sooner or later, consumed.

2. Notwithstanding these strictures on the doctrine which makes so many and important kinds of effort unproductive, there are still numerous instances of unproductive labor. The following are the most prominent of these : —

1. *Misdirected labor*, or that which does not secure the object at which it aims. If a man should devote months of time to the construction of a machine of which the mechanical principle on which it depends is impossible, his labor is, of course, ineffective.

2. All of that labor *the ultimate object of which is destruction*. Such almost wholly is war. It is admitted that wars may be waged to prevent a greater destruction than that involved in their prosecution. But, whatever may be the design of any war at the beginning, it must be acknowledged, that the destruction of wealth has been incalculably greater than the conservation or creation of it. Evidently most of the energy expended in war is unproductive. Here, too, must be reckoned the labor implied in maintaining vast standing armies. Could all this labor be turned into productive channels, it would incalculably augment the resources of the civilized world.

3. All *purely speculative projects*. By these I mean all such buying and selling as involve no increase of wealth to any one except by the same amount of diminution to others; in other words, where all that is gained by one party is necessarily lost by another. All trade which does not furnish some utility to society, not otherwise possessed, is unproductive.

4. Finally, we may rank here all labor expended in ministering to any desire the gratification of which will diminish the productive power of its subject, or of any under his

control. Such would include the manufacture and traffic in intoxicating beverages. Nor is this the only business which has this character, though doubtless it has it more obviously and conspicuously than any other. All the labor of furnishing a depraved literature to the perversion and enervation of the mind, and every system of effort by which is stimulated or gratified any passion or proclivity that diminishes man's power over himself, and so over the means which nature freely furnishes to all who are competent to command them, are of this kind.

CHAPTER IV.

CAPITAL.

1. WE have already seen that capital is essential to any considerable production. We have also seen that capital is the result of previous labor reserved to aid in future production. We have further learned that capital implies saving. But mere saving is not the sole condition of capital; indeed, a narrow penuriousness prevents the rapid accumulation of capital. The man who is accustomed to bring his water from a spring a quarter of a mile from his house, instead of digging a well at the cost of a few dollars or a few days' work, acts uneconomically. In the long-run, the bringing of the water from the spring costs him much more than the digging of the well. The man who has extensive grain-fields, and who, for the sake of saving the expense of a reaper or even a cradle, continues to use the sickle, will find that his saving results in a loss instead of a gain.

2. A man does not need to be rich in order to be a capitalist. When the savage has invented a bow and arrows, he has the rudiments of capital. The laborer who has reserved out of his earnings enough to buy him a set of tools, or a few acres of land, is as really a capitalist as the owner of factories and railroads. It is only as foresight discerns the valuable consequences of self-denial, that there arises a sufficient inducement to reserve from present consumption for future use. "The hardest lesson for children and savages to learn is that of economy,— the necessity of bridling the inclination or appetite of the moment, with a view to some prospective benefit. Long and hard experience has taught this lesson to the full-grown and reflecting man, and taught it so effectually, that, as is often the case, the acquired inclination overrides the original impulses; and all other passions are merged not merely in the love of accumulation, but in that of saving."[1]

3. Capital is not synonymous with wealth. It is only that portion of wealth which is employed in producing wealth. We need a little caution here, however, lest we be misled. There is a large amount of property which is not apparently or instantly productive, but which is unquestionably to be reckoned as capital. It furnishes certain conditions of production, inasmuch as, if it did not exist in its relation to the given enterprise, the latter could not go on. A farmer must have a considerable stock of provisions which he reserves from one harvest for his subsistence till another. These may lie a great part of the year inactive and apparently useless in his storehouses. But they are nevertheless a part of his capital, and without them his business must fail. The same is true of the fund which the manufacturer reserves with which to pay his workmen. It is the means of their subsistence between the time of their beginning work and the time when the completed product put in the market brings in its returns.

4. The difference between wealth and capital may be further illustrated. A man has a hundred thousand dollars. He decides to invest in a manufacturing enterprise. He expends a portion of it in buildings and their appurtenances adapted to his object. He reserves a sufficient amount for

[1] Professor Bowen.

the sustenance of laborers, which will be in the form of money to be paid out as wages; also a certain amount to be used in the purchase of raw material. He must also make provision for food, clothing, and shelter, to keep himself in a condition to do his own work till the time of returns from the products of the business. All this might properly be reckoned as capital. But the amount embraced in the last item must be strictly limited to the purposes designated; namely, to enable the proprietor to do the work essential to his business: otherwise it is not capital. If he does none of the work, but leaves the management to others, then the amount expended in food, clothing, and shelter is not capital at all. Or, if he be engaged in the business, all that he expends beyond what is essential to the purposes specified is so much outside of his capital. Thus he may put twenty thousand dollars into a house, grounds, gardens, conservatories, costly furniture, and works of art; but most of this is so much subtracted from his capital. It may be all properly and wisely used, but it is not used as a condition of further production.

5. Capital is divided into *fixed* and *circulating*. There are two distinct ways in which capital is applied to production. The main difference consists in this, that certain kinds of capital are used only once in the fulfilment of their purposes; certain other kinds are used repeatedly. There are also some minor differences.

Circulating capital is of two kinds. 1. There are the stock and commodities of any character to be consumed in reproduction. These embrace (*a*) the material out of which the new product is to come, — as lumber for cabinetware, leather for shoes, and cloth for garments; (*b*) food and other provisions for the sustenance of laborers. 2. There is the stock of completed commodities on hand and ready for the market. The chairs that are finished and ready for sale in the factory are of this character. It is to be observed, that the same article may be at one time circulating, and at another time fixed, capital. Thus the chairs just spoken of, while they are in the hands of the maker, or passing through the hands of the wholesale or retail dealer, are circulating capital. It is only when they become *fixed in use* that their character changes.

Fixed capital consists: 1. Of all tools, machinery, and implements used in any industry; under this head, too, are comprised all beasts of burden or draught, and all structures of every sort for manufacturing and productive purposes. 2. All improvements of land, such as clearing, draining, fencing, etc. 3. Mental acquisitions gained by labor, and which give man power for productive results.

6. It must be borne in mind, that there can be no production without consumption. All capital is consumed. This is readily seen in the case of circulating capital, but not so readily in that of fixed. Yet evidently tools, buildings, bridges, locomotives, and all other structures and instruments wear out. The only difference is, that in one case the consumption takes place at once; in the other, it is gradual. Some kinds of fixed capital are consumed more rapidly than others. The farmer's scythes, hoes, and hand-rakes rarely last more than a year or two. His carts, wagons, reapers, etc., last much longer. The steel pen with which I write these lines has been in use scarcely a week, and has now nearly exhausted its capability of service. The inkstand before me has served for nearly a dozen years. Some bridges and other structures have been in existence for centuries. The old Roman aqueducts are still seen stretching away for miles over the Campagna. Most of them, it is true, are in ruins; but the many yet remaining massive arches upholding the water-courses show how enduring are some of the products of human industry.

7. It is an interesting fact, and worthy of notice here, that nearly all the wealth now in existence has been created within a comparatively recent period, and most of it within a few years. We talk of property inherited from ancestors, as if it had been received from them in its present form. Many persons have the impression that no portion of the wealth of the community has been produced within the past year, except so much as may have been added to that previously existing. This is a great mistake. Says Mr. Mill, "The greater part in value of the wealth now existing in England has been produced within the last twelve months." This is stating the case pretty strongly, but it is not so far out of the way as one who has not investigated the subject might suppose. It is nearly certain that only a small proportion of the wealth now existing in England or in this country had any existence ten years ago. Capital is perpetuated, not by preservation in its present forms, but by continued reproduction.[1]

8. It will readily be seen that all fixed capital must have previously existed in the form of circulating capital, and that the former only results from the conversion of the latter. Thus, in the primitive condition of society, when the savage has secured a certain amount of food, he may consume that food at once, or he may reserve a certain portion of it till he has an accumulated store, on which he may then live while he takes time to construct an improved club, or a bow and arrows. In the latter case he has converted his

---

[1] The whole value of the industrial product of the United States for 1870 was estimated at $7,286,629,328. The whole value of all the property of the country was reputed by the same authority as a little more than $30,000,000,000. Thus the annual product was nearly one-fourth as much as the entire wealth.

means of sustenance, which was circulating capital, into fixed capital. By this means he has acquired additional power over nature, and can accumulate more rapidly than before. As he can now more easily supply his wants, he will, if the spirit of sacrifice be sufficiently strong, be able to contrive and invent other instruments which will always be the means of additional advantage in his contest with nature. It is this constant conversion of circulating into fixed capital, that marks the progress of man from barbarism to civilization, and the gradual predominance of mind over matter.

9. So far we see, in the case of a single individual and in the rudimentary condition of society, only good resulting from this change from the temporary into the permanent forms of wealth. This would seem to indicate a general law, that, in proportion as the tendency of property to take on permanent forms increases, the tendency to the growth of wealth increases; or, that capital increases with the tendency to the conversion of circulating into fixed capital.

Yet the opinion widely prevails among the uneducated or partially educated classes, and even to some extent among the better informed, that, as machinery is invented, more and more laborers will be thrown out of employment, and thus deprived of their means of support. There are many circumstances about the introduction of machinery, which, to a superficial observer, indicate such a consequence. Thus, on a certain large farm, twenty men have been necessary to do the harvesting. Now the proprietor purchases a reaper. With two horses and two or three men, as much can be accomplished as before with the whole twenty. Consequently seventeen or eighteen men are deprived of employment. In some instances of sudden and rapid invention and change, this would undoubtedly be the case. But these changes usually come on gradually. There is always a demand for a part of the displaced labor, in the construction of the machines. By reason of the increased facilities, there will be a larger production at the same cost. This will diminish the price, and greatly enlarge the demand, to satisfy which more laborers will be needed. There will also be a more rapid increase of capital, thus furnishing still additional opportunities for labor. The ultimate and not very remote result is, that more laborers are required than before the displacement, and that, too, at better wages; while, by means of the ever-increasing facilities, the cost of the means of living is diminished.

The inventions of Arkwright and Hargreaves, when they were first adopted, so alarmed and exasperated the poor spinners of the neighborhood, who looked upon them as portending starvation to themselves and their families, that they resorted to violence, and tore down the machinery, and drove away the inventors. Yet, I suppose, within the lifetime of these very workmen, and through the influence of these very machines, the demand for labor in the cotton-manufacture was more than doubled; while, for a great part of the time since, probably fifty times as many hands have been employed as previously. The increase of labor-saving machinery within the present century has been almost incalculable; yet wages have been almost constantly increasing, while such commodities as are desired by the laborers are constantly diminishing in value.

But while in general the conversion of circulating into fixed capital is not detrimental, but on the contrary advantageous to the laborer, there are exceptions. This conversion may take place at times and under conditions which render it an evil instead of a benefit. Instances of this are seen in the building of railroads through regions where there is no demand for them, or the multiplying of houses in a village or city where the increase of population does not warrant it. But these are mistakes which, while they do much mischief temporarily, yet quickly correct themselves from the very nature of the case.

CHAPTER V.

RELATIONS OF CAPITAL AND LABOR.

1. THE relation of capital and labor is, in general, that of mutual dependence. Capital can produce nothing without labor. Labor works at an immense disadvantage without capital. Doubtless the precedence must be given to labor, since it must have created the first capital, and is therefore competent to effect some rude production without capital. But each is essential to any considerable effectiveness of the other, and there is no real antagonism between them. The conflict of capitalists and laborers, so often manifested, arises out of the selfishness and ignorance of the human agents, and not out of the nature of things.

2. Labor is limited by capital. This is a fundamental proposition, but subject to various modifications. We have seen that capital of itself produces nothing. It only furnishes the conditions of successful labor. The capital upon which labor depends consists substantially of (a) the material to be wrought into other forms, (b) real estate, (c) machinery and implements, and (d) the sustenance of the workmen.

The proposition that labor is limited by capital is sometimes interpreted to mean, that, in any community with a given amount of capital, any increase of laborers must diminish the rate of wages, and that any increase of the rate must diminish the number of laborers employed. This interpretation presumes that all the capital of the community is employed in the most profitable manner, and that the labor applied to it is disposed according to the best methods. But these are conditions seldom likely to co-exist, even if they exist separately.

Still it remains true in general, that, when there is a small amount of capital, only a small amount of labor can be advantageously employed. On the other hand, the more capital there is, other things being equal, the greater will be the demand for labor, and the greater its remuneration.

3. Does the unproductive expenditure of the rich tend to the benefit of the poor by creating a demand for labor? This question has been much discussed, and even yet it is not with all minds clearly settled. Doubtless it does not admit of a categorical answer. The opinion that a profuse and extravagant consumption of wealth is beneficial to the community at large, can hardly be held without qualification by any person. Let us carefully consider the subject in several of its bearings.

Here is a man whose income is $20,000 a year. We will suppose that he consumes all this unproductively. He employs a large retinue of servants, he buys costly delicacies for his table, procures splendid furniture and expensive garments, and gives magnificent entertainments. All this expenditure may be for services rendered, — for the work of servants, the products of artisans and artists. It makes a demand for a large amount and a great variety of labor. But nearly all the product of all this labor is consumed within the year: nothing is reserved. It is true, if this is a permanent income, and this is our hypothesis, the same number of laborers, but no more, can be employed for the next and the subsequent years.

Now, suppose, that, instead of expending the whole $20,000, the proprietor had lived on $5,000. There would then have been $15,000 to add to the permanent capital of the community. This invested in business would have given employment to as many laborers as though it had been used in the other way. At the end of one year it may have little perceptible effect on the demand for labor; but, during the second year, this $15,000 reserved from the first year's income will be still in existence. There will be also the profit accruing from the investment. Instead of being wholly destroyed, as in the other case, it will now furnish opportunity for at least a few more laborers. If the proprietor continues to live on $5,000, and to employ the remainder of his income productively, there will be more than $30,000 to co-operate with labor, instead of the $20,000, as in the first instance. The next year this additional business-capital will exceed $45,000, and will soon go up to $60,000 and $100,000. Not only will there be a constantly increasing amount of capital, but, by the increase of production, commodities will be cheapened; and thus there will be a tendency both to an increase of wages and an enlargement of their purchasing power. Economy and not prodigality, on the part of the rich, is an advantage to the laborer.

CHAPTER VI.

SOME CONDITIONS OF HIGHEST PRODUCTION.

1. IT is only by the application of principles underlying political economy, that we come to the conditions of the highest production, or, in other words, find how to satisfy the largest range of desires, to the greatest extent, at the smallest cost of labor.

One great essential to this end is *the combination and division of labor*. It may seem strange that two apparently contradictory terms should represent entirely harmonious conceptions. But we shall see this to be actually the case.

We need at this point to recall what has already been said on the subject of *Association* and *Individuality*. We are made to be mutually dependent. From the cradle to the grave, most of our wants are supplied by others than ourselves. A full complement of human qualities is found only in the aggregate of humanity. Every one lacks something that some other can supply.

But in order to association, as we have seen, there must be difference. Two persons just alike would have no need of each other. Mutual dependence is in the inverse ratio of similarity. If one man be blind but otherwise physically sound, and another have good eyes but no legs, the blind man can carry the legless one on his shoulders; while the latter directs the former's course, and warns him of any danger or obstacle in the way. Two legless men would be of little use to each other, and "if the blind lead the blind, both shall fall into the ditch."

Association and *individuality* are the two characterizing forces of an advancing civilization. They are analogous to the centripetal and centrifugal forces in the physical world. Men combine to produce a certain result, because each can contribute something which another cannot so well or so readily. Hence combination is not only consistent with division of labor, but it is largely dependent upon it.

2. Combination or co-operation is of two kinds, — simple and complex. The former is illustrated in those instances in which several persons unite for the accomplishment of a result which could not be effected by separate workers except in much more than the proportionate time. There are also operations which can be performed by the combination of a number of persons, which one man could not effect in *any* length of time : such are the moving and placing of heavy timbers and stones, the management of ships and railway-trains, and many other such things.

Complex combination is where several persons help each other by following different employments. Each man needs nearly the same that every other man needs. But, while each provides for only one kind of want, he provides more than enough to satisfy his own desires in that particular respect, and contributes the overplus to meet that same want in others. As all others do the same, each is contributing to meet the desires of one, and all to each. The shoemaker, the tailor, the carpenter, the cabinet-maker, the blacksmith, the paper-maker, the tinman, the miner, the painter, etc., are all contributing to supply the farmer's needs ; and the farmer is as indispensable to the needs of all of them. The remarkable thing about it is, that most of these persons are working without any previous concert or mutual understanding, and are thus unconsciously co-operating for each other's advantage. The wants of each are many times more fully met in this way, than if each should undertake to supply all his own wants; since each can work to the best advantage if he confine himself to the few kinds of work for which he has taste and aptitude.

It is just here that we see the immense civilizing influence of this separation and co-operation in labor. Were every man compelled to produce for himself whatever he needs, it is evident that his provision for his needs would be meagre, and hardly obtained. The obstacles to acquisition would be so numerous, that, were he to put forth the most strenuous efforts, only a small part of what he might desire could be secured. No one would have any inducement to obtain much beyond the bare necessaries of life. There would be the scantiest accumulations, no capital worthy the name, and consequently no public works, scarcely any commerce, little culture, no art, science, or literature, — in a word, no civilization.

3. We have, so far, chiefly considered the separation of labor into different industries, each of which ministers to great numbers of the followers of other occupations. But, as civilization advances, the separation is carried further. In complicated trades the work is divided into a number of processes. The increase of the productive power of labor by this means is almost marvellous. The example of pin-making has been used as an illustration of this ever since Adam Smith. Formerly there were in this occupation eighteen distinct parts. An instance is given where only ten persons were employed, some of them performing two or three operations. With ordinary exertions they could make twelve pounds of pins in a day, or about forty-eight thousand pins

of average size. Each person, then, on an average, might be regarded as making forty-eight hundred in a day. But we are assured by those competent to judge, that if all had wrought separately, and none been educated to a particular process, they probably could not have made twenty pins apiece. This gives an increase, through combination and division, of *two hundred and forty fold.* Mr. Say gives an illustration from the manufacture of playing-cards, where the increase was two hundred and fifty-eight fold by the same method. This seems almost incredible, and yet there are so many other illustrations that there can be no doubt on the subject.

4. Among the benefits of the division of labor are the following: 1. The increase of dexterity in the workman. Persons of the commonest ability gain astonishing facility in a little time by concentrating upon one kind of action. A child fastening on the heads of pins, it is said, will repeat an operation requiring several distinct motions of the muscles, one hundred times a minute for several successive hours. Adam Smith states, that, if a blacksmith had to make nails without having been accustomed to the work, he would not make more than two or three hundred bad nails in a day. But boys who are brought up to that special work can turn out twenty-three hundred good nails in a day.

2. There is a saving of time and material. (*a*) In passing from one kind of work to another, much time is ordinarily lost. Neither the mind nor the muscles are ready for the new labor, and there is always more or less sauntering before getting adjusted to the changed conditions. It is true, however, that there is something of an offset in the fact, that, in such a change, a rest is afforded to one set of muscles while another set is called into action. (*b*) Time is saved, again, in learning the business. To master a com-

plicated trade might require, say, five years; but if the various processes be grouped in five divisions, and each of five men learn one of these in a year, and each devote himself to that which he learns, then twenty years of time will be saved in learning that trade by these five men. (*c*) There is also saving of material. In learning a trade, much material is commonly spoiled. If the diversity of operation be great, the waste will be proportionally great. This would be greater where each learns a whole trade than where only a single process is learned.

3. Another advantage is, that inventions to abbreviate or save labor in a particular department are more likely to occur to one whose attention is exclusively directed to that work.

4. A fourth advantage is so conspicuous and obvious that it is remarkable, that, instead of being the first noticed, it was not observed till among the last. It is that of classifying the laborers according to their capability. Different parts of a trade often require unequal degrees of skill and physical strength. By allowing those who have the least of these, to do the simpler and lighter parts of the work, the more complex, nicer, and heavier can be given to those more competent. The latter would not only do more work than if they ranged through the whole business, but they will do a portion which the former could not do at all, and would thus be unavailable as laborers. This exclusion of a large proportion of laborers would make the work much more costly. Take again the illustration of pin-making. Mr. Babbage has shown that some portions of this work require very considerable skill. Other portions can be performed by persons of ordinary ability, and in them young boys and girls often accomplish as much as experienced and skilled workmen. An instance is given where the wages ranged from six shillings a day down to four and one-half pence.

Now, if *all* these operations were to be performed by each laborer, only the six-shilling workmen could be employed, as they alone could do certain parts of the work. All the others would be shut out, the best workmen would get lower wages, and the cost of the product would be enhanced from five to ten fold.

5. There is also the advantage which comes from the multiplication of services. The express-companies, devoting themselves to the carrying of parcels and packages of goods, can carry a hundred or a thousand of these with many times less labor than all who have goods to send would have to expend did each carry his own.

6. The multiplication of copies, as is done by a printing-press, or in founderies, or by means of dies, is another example. To copy out by hand a thousand copies of the Bible or of Shakspeare, would cost five hundred or a thousand times as much as to have them printed where several copies are struck off from the same type.

5. But there are certain limitations to the divisions of labor. 1. One of these is the nature of the employment. Some occupations admit of only a certain number of divisions. In watch-making, it is said, there are more than a hundred distinct branches : in some other trades, only three or four are possible. Others still, while capable of manifold division, are such that the different kinds of work must be done at different seasons of the year, so that, if one made a speciality of any of these, he would needs be idle a good part of the time : of this kind is agriculture.

2. A second limitation is found in the demand for the product. A blacksmith setting up his forge in a sparsely settled neighborhood, the patronage of which will furnish occupation for only one man, must do all the different parts of the work himself. If the community increases, he may

employ an apprentice; and continued growth may furnish occasion for a journeyman, and perhaps more than one, and the divisions take place accordingly.

3. Another limitation is in the amount of capital employed in the business. Where there is but little capital, the proprietor can employ but few workmen. He can purchase but a small stock of material, and his supply of tools and apparatus must necessarily be small. He can in such case set only a limited number of men to work, even if he could advance the amount necessary for their wages. Consequently, there can be but a small division of labor.

6. There are some disadvantages as well as advantages in the division of labor. 1. Such subdivisions of employment have a tendency to impair physical health. They afford too little variety of muscular exertion. While this is not universally the case, it is too often so. There is the constant pressure upon certain portions of the body, and none upon others. There is a want of balance. There are also certain processes which require an unnatural position, which, if long continued, is likely to induce deformity and perhaps disease. This liability, though perhaps less than it is sometimes made to seem, is still actual, and demands consideration.

2. It diminishes the self-reliance of laborers. It is apt to generate a feeling of dependence, since the worker may acquire the habit of expecting others to do almost every thing for him. One comes to regard one's self as only an element in a great system, — a small portion of a machine, which, as a whole, produces certain results. There are, doubtless, exceptional instances, in which separation of employment develops individuality; but it oftener has the opposite effect.

Closely connected with this is the consequence that the number of those who do business on their own account is diminished. It is not well that the proprietors in a community should be few. Ownership, responsibility, the conciousness of being one's own master, foster manliness, and tend to the development of character. It is true, if all men were proprietors, the interests of industry might suffer; but if only a *very few* were such, it would suffer still more. We should seek as far as possible to avoid the evils incident to either extreme.

3. A third disadvantage, though closely connected with the second, is more serious than either of the others. In the minute subdivisions which characterize our modern industry, there is a hinderance to mental growth, — a contracting and belittling influence hard to resist. When a workman works all day, and day after day, boring holes or turning spindles, or cutting the same patterns with a jig-saw, it requires much effort both in and out of work-hours to keep the mind from a deterioration of which it is sad to think. I can scarcely conceive how any man of even moderate intelligence can be content to confine himself for any considerable time to such sterile operations. It is true, that, under the conditions which such division of labor implies, there are found certain compensations. First, by this means, men are brought into communication with one another more than they would otherwise be. Information is thus gained, inquiries suggested, and thought excited. All this is every way wholesome. Secondly, the very fact that many of these minute operations can be performed with but little draught on the mind, and some of them almost automatically, implies mental leisure in which thought can go on simultaneously with work. If the vacant hours be only moderately improved, culture and development need not be wholly wanting.

CHAPTER VII.

CONDITIONS OF HIGHEST PRODUCTION (*continued*).

1. CLOSELY connected with the subject of combination and division of labor, is that of the *diversification of industry*. Upon this depends to no small extent the measure of the productiveness of a community. There is a somewhat prevalent doctrine which is antagonistic to this. It is, that the principle of the division of labor should apply to separate communities, as well as to the different individuals of the same community. This doctrine is more frequently implied than explicitly stated.

It is obvious enough, that each community should devote itself to such industries as it can on the whole pursue to the best advantage; that it should not cherish those which it cannot thus pursue. In other words, no industry should be supported *merely* for the sake of the industry. But neither, on the other hand, should distribution of industries to different communities be practised for the sake of this distribution. It is obvious, that, in proportion as such a distribution takes place, there must be a diminution of the diversity in each several community. If each society should confine itself to the production of two or three commodities, it must depend on other societies to furnish it with most of the articles which it may need. It has already been shown that the association, combination, and commerce, so essential to the prosperity if not to the existence of a community, can exist only where there are differences; and that these differences must exist in part in modes and forms of production. Hence to locate the differing individuals in separate communities, and to cultivate a similarity in each, would be to put commerce at a disadvantage, and to rob men of the vast benefits of one chief element of their constitution.

2. In every considerable community there are a great number of diverse tastes and aptitudes, many of which cannot be easily adjusted except to particular employments; and unless these exist, a large proportion of the labor-force will be either unapplied, or so applied as to lose much of its legitimate effect.

It is not only that more and better work will be done, and therefore that greater productiveness will ensue, but there are a thousand things done which would otherwise fail of accomplishment, and a thousand things utilized which would otherwise be wasted. A manufacturing community in the midst of an agricultural region not only furnishes immediate exchange which must otherwise be sought at great expense of time and transportation, but it furnishes a market for scores of commodities which, remote from such a community, would be substantially valueless. Few are aware how great is the number of objects which at a distance from towns and cities are comparatively useless, but which in their immediate vicinity would constitute a source of wealth.

Agriculture, in an extended section where it is nearly the exclusive business, is ever an employment of diminishing profit. The land wears out, and the waste both of labor and capital is prodigious. It is a remarkable fact, that famines are more frequent and more appalling in exclusively or chiefly agricultural regions than anywhere else. We can hardly conceive of a famine as possible in our Eastern States or in England; but in the most fertile regions of the West, twice within the last twenty-five years there have been extensive and disastrous famines. This is necessarily incidental to an exclusively agricultural community. If there be but a single staple production, and that fails, the entire resources fail; but if there be many industries, not all nor even a majority of them are likely to collapse at the same time.

But this is only one aspect of the evil implied in a small number of industries. A doctrine already presented is, that no one occupation furnishes scope for more than a small fraction of the varied talent existing in a community. "If four millions are obliged to be rude laborers, when three millions of them might be skilled artisans, the labor of one of the latter being supposed to be equal in value to three of the former, then the value actually created is to the value which might be created as four is to ten: in other words, the yearly product of the national industry might be two and a half times greater than it is, and the yearly unproductive consumption need not be at all increased; since, in either case, there would be four millions of people to be supplied with food and clothing and shelter."[1]

3. Another condition of increased production is unrestricted labor, and freedom of competition. But this freedom must be real and practical, not merely theoretical. The power of the members of the community to associate must not be hindered, in order to the healthy circulation previously mentioned. To assure and preserve this freedom, is one of the functions of government. It should protect each member of society against fraud and violence. It cannot furnish labor, or create capital; it cannot repeal the laws of nature, or enact new ones. But it may guard against

[1] Bowen's Political Economy, pp. 84, 85.

the destruction of the operation of these laws by artificial and vicious measures devised by selfish men. It may do something, at least, to discourage and limit combinations which would attempt to monopolize advantages in the interest of the few, to the exclusion of the many for whom they were intended, — schemes to prevent free and natural competition, and to force labor and capital into unnatural channels, to the detriment of the great masses of producers and consumers. It may take any available means to thwart any movement of interested foreign parties to overwhelm and destroy the nascent industries of its own citizens, as they come into competition with those of the former.

4. An important condition of increasing productiveness is found in *general education*. The utility of education in its relation to human society is twofold. First, a certain degree of intelligence in the masses of the citizens is essential to the success, or even the existence, of a republican form of government. But the discussion of the subject in this respect belongs rather to the department of civil polity than to that of political economy.

The economical advantage of education consists in the skill, discernment, and discrimination which it gives a man for his work; the ability to adapt means to ends; and, in a word, power over nature, so that he can the more readily avail himself of her resources, and command her services. Obviously every increase of this power is an increase of productive capability.

It has always been admitted, that such native or acquired intellectual ability as enables one to discover new forces in nature, or to apply these in the industries, or to make new combinations of forces already known, is a vast and valuable aid to production. Not less is the estimate to be put on the talent to organize and manage great business enterprises, so as to make the co-operation of labor and capital in them advantageous. Yet it is probable that the benefits thus resulting from education have been largely underestimated. The increase of power furnished by nature through the discoveries of science, and through human invention, is altogether incalculable. The steam-power of Great Britain, years ago, was estimated to be equal to the labor of six hundred millions of men. Thus in one little island, containing less than one-fortieth of the population of the earth, there has been developed a mechanical power equal to nearly or quite the whole human working-force of the planet! This is only one of the contributions to human productiveness by educated mind. Yet much of this discovery comes from moderately educated men engaged in manual labor.

There is another fact concerning education in relation to labor, which is worthy of note. It is, that the most ordinary education adds to the efficiency of the most ordinary laborer. Even a ditch-digger will do better work by reason of a rudimentary education. In all the rising grades of employments, the more intelligent the laborer, — other things being equal, — the more effective the labor. Usually, too, when the laborer is even moderately educated, he is more likely to be frugal and prudent; and, while producing more, he saves a larger part of that which is produced, thus effecting a double increase of the capital of the community. It also adds to his self-respect, and furnishes a motive to seek a competence and independence, and so, in several ways, contributes to the end for which it has inspired the hope.

It is true, that, as education increases, the desires of men multiply, and the consumption will be greater. But consumption will increase less rapidly than production from this cause. Then, too, the increased desires are in themselves a stimulus to exertion, and tend to create a larger demand for the results of labor. Thus there is no assignable limit to the multiplication of human desires creating a demand for those results of human effort whereby these desires are gratified.

5. Finally, the productiveness of a community depends in no small degree on the *moral character* of its members. In order to any considerable productiveness, as we have seen, there must be association, combination, and mutual dependence. In order that these may exist, men must have confidence in each other. There must be individual honor, integrity, fidelity, or this cannot exist. Then, again, unless there be security for property, men will have neither much inducement to labor nor much incentive to save in order to accumulate capital. In proportion as morality is at a low grade, as fraud and violence are rife, or as peculation and swindling prevail among officials, and public trusts are betrayed, will enterprise languish, capital seek safer localities, and thriftless poverty become the characteristic of the community. On the other hand, where integrity and uprightness abound in the society, there will be security to property, capital will not need to be so vigorously hedged about with expensive safeguards, labor will superintend itself at a great saving of cost, and all the interests of the community will feel the favorable effect.

BOOK SECOND.

CONSUMPTION.

CHAPTER I.

THE NATURE AND THE VARIOUS FORMS OF CONSUMPTION.

1. Consumption is the destruction of values. Production implies consumption. In general, all material is destroyed in entering into new forms of wealth. Thus leather must be destroyed in order to produce shoes. Flour must disappear in the manufacture of bread, and wheat in the making of flour. Every kind of implement or machine or structure is consumed by use. This consumption may be immediate (that is, by a single use), or it may be gradual. The fuel that we burn and the food that we eat are examples of the former; tools, bridges, buildings, and aqueducts are examples of the latter. The consumption may be accomplished in a few days or months, or it may be protracted through centuries.

2. The value which disappears in consumption is not necessarily lost. The value of the leather which the shoemaker destroys re-appears in the shoes. The value of the lumber, stone, and brick consumed by the builder is reproduced in the house. The seed which is cast into the soil utterly perishes, but it furnishes conditions of a value much greater than that which is destroyed.

It is in this way that wealth increases; not merely by adding to the valuable things already existing, but by destroying many of these that there may issue still greater value.

The prosperity of a nation is not inversely as the consumption of values, nor is it precisely the opposite. Still, if there is very little consumption, there is very little increase of value.

3. Consumption is either *voluntary* or *involuntary*. The former is exemplified in the instances heretofore noticed, where man destroys one commodity either for the purpose of producing another, or for the purpose of immediate gratification. Of the latter, we have instances in the natural decay of objects, as the rusting of iron, the mildew of cotton and woollen fabrics, and the wearing away, by attrition, of gold, silver, and other metals; also the destruction caused by vermin. Much of this may be prevented by the prudent foresight which sound economy enjoins, but much loss will inevitably take place. A great deal of consumption comes by what is called *accident*. Much destruction is caused by fires, steam-boiler explosions, floods and tornadoes, earthquakes and volcanic eruptions.

CHAPTER II.

PRODUCTIVE AND UNPRODUCTIVE CONSUMPTION.

1. VOLUNTARY consumption is either productive or unproductive. The former is when the material appears in a new form and with higher value, as cloth made into garments, and iron into hardware and cutlery. Unproductive consumption occurs both in the instances previously mentioned, — of consumption by natural decay, and that which comes by accident, — and in cases where gratification of desire is the sole object sought and achieved, as when one eats and drinks simply for enjoyment, and without reference to the repair of nature's waste or the nourishment of the system.

It is not always easy to discriminate between these two kinds of consumption. We readily see the difference between a man's drinking a quantity of whiskey, — not because it will help in the performance of any work, but because he likes it, — and the scattering of a quantity of seed over the ground in the spring. There is no doubt that one of these acts is productive, and the other unproductive. But there are cases where the distinction is less clear.

It is not necessarily a case of unproductive consumption, when one destroys value for the sake of gratifying some desire. Probably a majority of men eat and drink simply because they desire food, having no thought of any ulterior object. Yet this eating and drinking are absolutely essential to productive labor. The wealth consumed in this way re-appears, to a large extent, in the products of human industry.

2. Still there is much really unproductive consumption,— a destruction of value in the place of which no other value appears. There are, for instance, men and women

> "who creep
> Into this world to eat and sleep,
> And know no reason why they're born,
> But simply to consume the corn."

Vast quantities of wealth are consumed in riotous living, in greedy and vulgar extravagance, and unmeaning magnificence. There is also much consumption designed to be productive, but failing of its end through misdirection. In these ways, much wealth is consumed, with no consequent product.

3. It is not always easy to draw the line between the conveniences of life and its luxuries; nor can the extent to which the latter, in any sense of the term, are allowable, be precisely indicated. What to one class of persons may be a luxury, to another class may be almost a necessity. So what might in one age have been a rare and expensive indulgence, is in an advanced age among the most ordinary conveniences. I call special attention to three kinds of consumption.[1]

1. There is the consumption necessary to life and the performance of productive labor. The word *necessary* is used here in its liberal, rather than its restricted, sense. The absolute necessities of human life are very few. It does not even require much to keep a man in working condition. But to keep him where there is a larger kind of living, and

[1] See Ruskin's Political Economy of Art.

where his energies of both body and mind, together with the moral qualities which render him the most efficient, are at their best, the consumption must be somewhat more generous.

Besides subsistence, there must be materials, tools, and a variety of conditions involving the destruction of value. It is desirable to sustain a man, not as a mere savage, but to give him the largest possible volume of human life; and the civilized man, it will be admitted, lives a broader life than the savage. We are not to forget that the object of political economy is rather to enhance the value of man than the multiplication of material wealth or the increase of commerce, except as the latter are conditions of the former.

2. A second kind of consumption is of such articles as minister to physical enjoyment, and meet a certain low order of mental appetencies. They are not essential to sustain life, or to render it more efficient. On the contrary, they often impair the vigor and competence of the person. At the best they simply gratify certain desires, without adding any thing to the value of the man. To this category belong mere dainty food; gold and jewels, and other ornaments worn for their showiness and not for any artistic excellence; gay and costly apparel, in which the gayety and costliness are the main features. These constitute a class of luxuries that are in every sense non-productive. They favorably affect neither the individual nor society, and are, for the most part, hurtful to both.

3. But not all consumption, the object of which is to gratify desire, is to be reckoned in this category. There are certain pleasures which ennoble and really enrich those who participate in them. There are desires, the gratification of which enlarges the volume of one's being. They are related not so much to man's productive capability as to that

which is the final cause of all production, and to which all wealth is only a means. The labor, materials, implements, and whatever else is consumed in the production of the works or effects of genuine art, result in the most real wealth that exists. By this is meant not merely pictures, statues, books, carved work, tasteful tapestries, and similar objects which can be bought and sold; but also oratorios which may be heard but once; magnificent parks, to which you may be admitted, but which you may never own; great actors and singers, whose genius may be exhibited to others, but not possessed by them. It is true, that much which properly belongs here may be so consumed as to deserve only a place in the second class; but it may also have those higher and nobler uses which imply production in the best sense.

CHAPTER III.

PUBLIC CONSUMPTION.

1. PUBLIC consumption is the expenditure of means for society in its aggregate capacity. It has reference principally to the cost of the operation of those agencies which are implied in the term *government*. The reasons for the necessity of such expenditure have already been given. The purposes to which such consumption properly contributes may be grouped as follows: —

(*a*) The support and administration of government. This embraces compensation to executive, legislative, and judicial officers, and expenditure for public buildings. (*b*) Works of public convenience. Here are included the paving and lighting of streets, water-works, sewerage, the light-house system, and some others. (*c*) For the purpose of advancing science and promoting intelligence by means of exploring expeditions, geological surveys, meteorological and astronomical observations, etc. (*d*) The promotion of popular education. (*e*) The support of the poor, and relief of the afflicted. (*f*) The national defence.

2. It would scarcely be possible to lay down any very definite general rule respecting the expenditures economically allowable for any of the above purposes. Still some limitations may be indicated.

As to the compensation which an officer of the government should receive, there has been some difference of opinion. On the one hand, it has been urged that it should be large and liberal; on the other, that it should be of such a moderate amount as would in itself be no temptation to any to seek the office. Some claim that the honor and respect which is attached to a position of public trust is in itself a considerable remuneration. No doubt there is, in a certain sense, something in this. In Great Britain, members of Parliament serve without pecuniary reward. But it has been well said, that to require men who by education, character, and experience are competent to serve the public gratuitously, or with no other reward than the honor and respect attached to the office, is to throw all such offices into the hands of the rich and those who are able to give their time to the public. In this way some, at least, of the best talent for the direction of public affairs would be excluded from participation in the government. The men who are pecuniarily able to render gratuitous public service comprise a comparatively small class, and the number of them possessing the highest order of ability is not likely to be sufficient for the duty required.

What has been said on the question of any salary is applicable to that of a large or a small salary. The compensation should at least be such as the same ability would command in any other equally important business. But it must also be considered, that a man in a public office, especially if it be a prominent one, is obliged to adopt a somewhat more expensive style of living than one in a private station. There is a dignity appropriate to such a situation, with which the expenditures of the incumbent will properly enough be expected to correspond. Under a republican form of government, the demand for this is less imperative than under a monarchy; and, under any form of government, it is liable to be carried to excess. Still some consideration is due to it. There should be neither meanness on the one hand, nor extravagance on the other. There should always be such salaries as will command the best abilities; and these should be secured on their own account, and the officer held to the same accountability as a person in any other responsible position.

What shall be the limit of expenditures in the construction of public buildings? About one point, there can be little dispute. There should be the least possible expense compatible with the largest possible advantage. One extreme would be the cheapest structures which could be made to answer for the transaction of the public business. They would be built in the plainest style, and with no regard to art or beauty. The opposite extreme would be to make them extravagantly costly and magnificent, till the main design would be lost sight of in the splendor of the adornments. There is a mean somewhere between niggardliness on the one hand and expensive ostentation on the other. It is for a nation, as well as for an individual, to make a reasonable use of art; and it is not essential to public economy that the public expenses should be only in the line of the necessary and the ordinary.

3. The propriety of public expenditure for the purpose of general education has been incidentally but pretty fully discussed in its relation to production. It is evident, if there is to be to any considerable extent an education for the masses, the expense of it must be borne by the community as a whole. It is scarcely possible to consider the subject in any of its bearings except, in part at least, under this aspect. The duty of the government, as the agent of the whole society; the necessity of education to the existence and permanence of popular government; the moral consequences, on the one hand, of its encouragement, and, on the other, of neglecting it; and the vast economical benefit resulting from it, — are so universally recognized among us, that it is unnecessary to add to what has been said.

Closely connected with expenditures for education are those for the promotion of scientific discovery and the diffusion of intelligence. Very many of the expeditions, investigations, and other measures for these purposes, are of a character which would prevent their being carried forward by private parties. The results which come from them are of vast benefit, not merely to some particular class, but to the community as a whole. Our own government sometimes, through these agencies, performs services the value of which to our own country is a hundred-fold greater than that consumed in their maintenance.

4. The question of *pauperism* is one of serious interest in all our modern communities. It is true that the theories of certain writers imply that it is not a matter pertaining to political economy at all, but rather one of benevolence and charity, such as a nation, in its corporate capacity, cannot be supposed to exercise. Some hold that the public support of the poor who are made so by the increase of population beyond the increase of capital, or who have become so by improvidence, is an interference with the laws of nature and the Divine appointments. But, however positive these teachers are in asserting such theories, few of them would be forward in putting them in practice. For they are not inhumane men: it is only one instance among many where men are better than their creeds.

But it is not difficult to show, that, to a certain extent, the public support of those who are not able to support themselves is a matter of *economy*, as well as of charity. In any case it is certain that no civilized community can be found in our day, where, whether prompted by humanity or by some other impulse, help will not be forthcoming to the unfortunate. Since this is so, the question is, how to make the provision as effectual as possible, and at as little cost. In many nations, there is no general arrangement by the government for the relief of the needy. There mendicancy takes the place of pauperism, and is unquestionably far more expensive as well as far more deleterious. In these nations, as in most others, there are various eleemosynary institutions, whose object is to relieve the needy. Provision is also made, to some extent, by churches and mutual-aid societies and benevolent associations. But after all that private beneficence can do, even when most efficiently organized, there will still be many cases which it cannot reach.

Of the method of relief, a few words must suffice. It is obviously better that the system of caring for the poor should be local; that is, it should pertain to the cities, towns, or counties, rather than to any larger political divisions. It is hardly possible for the government of any extensive territory to ascertain, and properly treat, the poor of every locality. But the authorities of a town or of a city ward can more easily comprehend the wants of those within their own limits, and relieve their wants with better adaptations and greater economy, than could be done by a general government.

5. The greatest and most ruinous consumption that takes place, in a palpable way, is that which is implied in *war*. If there is not more actual and ruthless waste of wealth in this than in any other way, it is at least more direct and obvious here than elsewhere. Without taking time to discuss the methods by which wars may be prevented, it may be admitted, that, in the present moral condition of humanity, war is a possibility to which any nation is liable. Self-defence is

a law of society, as well as of individual being. Hence all nations are expected to repel foreign invasions, and to repress domestic insurrection. All force used in the execution of the laws is war in embryo. It follows, then, that the vast expenditures for war are not in every case uneconomical. When forced upon a nation by the alternative of subjugation or vigorous self-defence, the expenditures for this purpose are as legitimate as those of the government for any other purpose.

The liability to such a condition, too, implies the propriety of a constant preparation for it. Indeed, this is one of the means of preventing it. This implies military defences, as forts and fortifications; also, collections of all sorts of arms and materials in arsenals and military depots. There must be at least the nucleus of an army, if not a considerable number of armed men, even in time of peace; and, in any case, such an enrolment of able-bodied men, and such encouragement of military training, as will furnish the elements of an effective soldiery. To this end, too, there must be military and naval schools for the education of men competent to become officers and engineers. There must be vessels of war, navy-yards, and the armament and material implied in these. The costliness is very great: it forms an important part of the expenditure of every government.

But while so much is admitted, there is in many countries an expenditure in this respect which is almost incredibly uneconomical. In the five great nations of Europe, the number and cost of the standing armies, as gathered from the statistics of a few years ago, are about as follows. In Austria the army consists of 280,000 men, and costs $45,000,000 a year. France has an army of 430,000, at a cost of about $100,000,000. The German Empire maintains a force of 420,000, at a cost of nearly $90,000,000. Great Britain has

200,000 men, costing $70,000,000. Russia has 800,000, at a cost of about $117,000,000.

Here, then, we have in five nations, and *in time of peace*, more than 2,000,000 men, comprising, of course, the most vigorous and valuable men in their several communities, taken from the ranks of productive industry, and, instead of adding to the wealth of the community, subtracting from it by large unproductive consumption. Four of these nations support heavy naval establishments, involving additional vast expenditures, and the absorption of many men.

Book Third.

EXCHANGE.

CHAPTER I.

PRINCIPLES WHICH FORM THE BASIS OF EXCHANGE.

1. *Exchange is the mutual and voluntary transfer of the right of property held by different persons.* This definition implies three things: 1. That there is such a thing as *a right of property*. This right is universally acknowledged, except by a few extremists and doctrinaires. It arises from the creation of value through labor. The advantage thus achieved naturally belongs to the parties putting forth the labor, if it be the result of their labor alone. If this labor be united with capital in the production, then a proportionate part belongs to the laborer, and the remainder to the owner of the capital. Each owner has the right to transfer his ownership to another. 2. In order to an exchange, this transfer must be *mutual*. If only one of the parties makes a transfer, and there is no consideration, it is a gift. 3. It must also be *voluntary*. If one is forced to relinquish one's right, it may be robbery: it is not exchange.

2. The one great and essential want of man is *association*. We are created with divers abilities, tastes, and aptitudes. These constitute our *individuality*, which, as we have seen, is not only compatible with association, but necessary to it. It is the very diversity of human character which makes men dependent on one another, and thus renders association indispensable. It is this general principle which underlies exchange. It is the same as that which gives rise to the combination and division of labor in production. There are usually some very few kinds of labor to which each individual is adapted. Yet the variety of productive work is so great that each may easily find some place in which to exercise his particular gift. But, while man is thus limited in his individual productive capabilities, his desires and wants are almost limitless. Each can produce much more of one commodity than he can use ; but he can and will, if possible, consume many more than he can produce. He can create a single kind of value : he desires a thousand kinds. Hence arises exchange. It is this which makes human society. Commerce is a necessity of man's nature : it is the means that binds up together, and holds in harmony, the multifarious elements and interests of a community.

3. The same general principles govern in exchanges between nations and remote communities. Yet it is to be noted and particularly considered, that the diversity existing between individuals must be greater than that between communities. The reasons for this have already been given. That the majority of individual occupations should exist in each community, rather than be distributed among several, is obvious. Yet God has so ordered, that there are natural diversities in nations, as well as in individuals. Every nation has some capability or facility which no other has.

4. The words *commerce* and *trade* are, in common conversation and by most writers, used as nearly synonymous and interchangeable. Mr. Carey makes a clear, and, as it seems to me, a reasonable distinction between these terms, and assigns to each a peculiar meaning. *Commerce* he defines as the intercourse of men with each other in the exchange of services, commodities, or ideas. *Trade* is the business of making exchanges *for* others. Commerce is the *object* sought

to be accomplished: trade is the *agency* by which it is accomplished.

There are certain obstacles to direct exchange, which cannot be surmounted except by some kind of intermediate agency, and this makes the trader necessary. In this respect and to this extent, trade aids instead of antagonizing commerce. It is certainly better for the community, that there be places of resort where every one is likely to find that of which he is in want, than to have to seek it among a variety of producers. Especially is this the case if the article is not produced in the vicinity. So, also, if one have an article of which he wishes to dispose, it is better to have some place where he is practically sure of finding a purchaser, than to spend days in the search for one. But the greater the number of commodities produced among themselves, and which are needed by members of the same community, the fewer will be the traders necessary to be employed, and the less costly will be the process of exchange.

CHAPTER II.

THE LAW OF EXCHANGE.

1. THE general law of exchange is *value for value*. This is implied in one of our previous statements concerning the essential nature of value; namely, that it is the quantity of one commodity which may be equitably exchanged for a given quantity of another. It will be still more clearly seen if we recall our final definition: *Value is our estimate of the sacrifice requisite to secure the possession of a desired object.* This sacrifice, as we have seen, usually involves both labor and abstinence. It is sometimes spoken of as the *cost of production*, though the meaning of this expression is somewhat modified in use. But the amount of labor implied in the production of a commodity is primarily and substantially what is meant by its cost.

Now, when two commodities come into the market, they will exchange for each other in quantities which will be inversely as the cost of production. If it require the labor of one day to produce a pair of shoes, and the labor also of a day to produce three bushels of oats, then the rule of exchange would be three bushels of oats for a pair of shoes. If it costs as much to produce sixty pounds of wheat, and bring it to the market, as it does to produce and bring to the market five pounds of beef, then the value of the latter is the same as that of the former; and they may be equitably exchanged for each other. This is the natural rule, and this is what is meant by value for value.

2. There are, however, various conditions which modify the operation of this law. The chief of these arises from the relations of supply and demand to normal value. Of these I shall speak hereafter. At present, let us recall the fact that value is a relative term. For this reason, there can be no such thing as a *general rise or fall of values*. If the value of any one thing rises or falls, that of something else must do the opposite. If all commodities are put in two classes, the value of one being expressed in terms of the other, they cannot both lose or gain at the same time, any more than the two arms of a balance can ascend or descend at the same time. If the value of the one is increased, the value of the other is diminished in an exactly corresponding ratio. So, if the value of thirty or forty or a hundred articles change, there must be a corresponding opposite change in the value of some other article or articles. If the value of the aggregate of all commodities save one be diminished, the value of that one will be increased in the exact corresponding ratio. It makes no difference whether this be leather or cloth or wheat or *money*.

3. We now come to consider *supply and demand* in relation to value. The natural value of a commodity is that which corresponds with the cost of its production: it is the central value, or that toward which the market value is "constantly gravitating, and any deviation from which is but a temporary irregularity, which, the moment it exists, sets forces in motion tending to correct it. On an average of years sufficient to enable the oscillations on one side the central line to be compensated by those on the other, the market value agrees with the natural value; but it very seldom agrees with it at any particular time. The sea everywhere

tends to a level, but it never is at an exact level. Its surface is always ruffled by waves, and often agitated by storms. It is enough that no point, at least in the open sea, is permanently higher than another. Each point is alternately elevated and depressed; but the ocean preserves its level."[1]

In attributing to supply and demand the cause of this fluctuation of values, is implied the necessity of explaining these terms, not merely in their intrinsic signification, but in their relation to each other. To define them superficially, as applied to commercial affairs, is not difficult. Thus *supply* may be regarded as the total amount of any particular commodity which is in the market, and *demand* as the total amount which the community desires to purchase. If there is more than the usual amount offered for sale, there will ordinarily be a competition among the sellers; and, as each would sell at something less than the usual profit, or, if it be a speedily perishable article, at no profit, or even at some loss, rather than lose the whole, there will be a diminution of prices, that is, of value expressed in money. On the other hand, if there be, for any reason, in the community an enlarged desire to purchase the commodity referred to, while the amount offered for sale remains the same, there will be a competition among the buyers; some, at least, being willing to give more than the ordinary price rather than forego its possession. Hence prices will rise.

The law of supply and demand derived from the foregoing observation is very simple. Other things being equal, 1. The greater the supply, the less the price; 2. The smaller the supply, the greater the price; 3. The greater the demand, the greater the price; 4. The smaller the demand, the less the price; and, generally, the price will vary directly as the demand, and inversely as the supply.

[1] Mill's Principles of Political Economy, vol. i. p. 557.

4. But, in order to a thorough understanding of the subject, more careful examination is required. In the superficial statement previously made, supply represents a *quantity*, and demand a *desire*. But the quantity represented by supply is not always the quantity in existence, but the quantity in the market. Now, not only does the quantity in the market affect the price, but the price affects the quantity in the market. If a farmer bring a load of wheat to market, expecting to sell it at a dollar a bushel, but finds that the price is only ninety cents, he may on that account withdraw it from the market, thus diminishing the supply. In other words, so long as the price is one dollar, the farmer's load is a part of the supply; but at ninety cents the supply is smaller by the amount of that load. Here diminution of price has diminished supply.

So, by the statement previously made, the prominent element in demand is *desire*. But, obviously, mere desire for a commodity does not constitute commercial demand for it. In a town of five thousand inhabitants, there may be a thousand persons who desire diamonds. But there is no demand to this extent; since probably not a hundred, and perhaps not a score, have the ability to purchase diamonds. Hence the meaning of demand is modified to *desire with ability to purchase*. This is sometimes called " effectual demand."

5. But here another phenomenon presents itself. Let us suppose a commodity of such cost that only persons who have an income of two thousand dollars a year can afford to purchase it. By some improvement in the facilities of production, the supply is doubled. According to the general law, the price will fall. Possibly it falls so much as to come within the reach of those whose income is one thousand dollars. Here, evidently, the demand is increased by the diminution of the price. But by the general law the increase of

demand increases the price. In this case, as in that of supply, the law is met by a counter law. Another interesting fact emerges here. The diminution of the price has increased the demand to the extent that not only those with an income of two thousand dollars can purchase it, but also those with an income of one thousand dollars. As the latter class is several times more numerous than the former, it follows that the demand is several times larger than when the higher price ruled. This will again increase the price, which will ascend till it reaches a point where only those having an income somewhere between one and two thousand dollars can afford to purchase. This, then, is the general law of prices: they tend to seek the level of the cost of production. When demand and supply from any cause become unequal, the natural competition of both labor and capital immediately operates to restore the equilibrium.

6. So far we have been considering cases where the supply is not restricted, and the production interrupted, by extraneous causes. There are cases, however, where such limitations do exist so that there can be either no immediate increase, or really no increase at all. As an instance of the former, suppose a community in which the crop of grain has been cut off so that there is only one-half or one-third the usual amount, which usual amount was just adequate to the wants of the people. If the community is so separated from the rest of the world that importation is out of the question, it is plain, there can be no increase of the quantity till the next year. In such a case, there would be a great rise of prices, with no corrective principle to restore the natural level.

There is another case where the supply is absolutely limited, not for a season only, but forever. There are certain commodities, to the number of which there can be no possible addition. Such are works of art by famous masters now dead, antique coins, rare volumes long out of print and impossible of imitation, and manuscripts of ancient documents. Of such, the cost of production furnishes no standard of value whatever. If two or three pictures by Raphael or Murillo or Titian were offered for sale in one of our great cities, thousands of persons might desire to possess one of them; but only a very few could do so. If put up at auction, the prices offered by the mass of those who would like to secure them would soon be surpassed by those offered by a small number. This number would be quickly reduced to fifty, then to thirty, to twenty, to ten, and finally to a number equal to the number of pictures for sale; that is, to a number where the supply was just equal to the demand at so high a price.

7. Supply and demand operate in still other ways, and are affected by other causes, than those already mentioned.

1. If there be a suddenly enlarged demand for a commodity not readily admitting of increased production, the price will be likely to rise more rapidly, and to a higher point, than in cases of continuous production and readily multiplied facilities for enlarging the supply. There are articles of which only a limited quantity is kept on hand and for sale in a community of moderate numbers, and which are produced at some distance from the place of consumption. Thus, in a small way, we may have seen this exemplified, when, in the late autumn or early winter, there is but little wood in a village or town, and the roads are so bad that for weeks scarcely any can be hauled from the country. The price will increase more, and more rapidly, than when the scarcity is one the anticipation of which would bring considerable quantities to the market.

2. It also makes a difference whether the article be a

necessary or only a luxury. If it be the former, the price will rise higher and more rapidly than if it were the latter. A man will double and treble his payment for bread, rather than go hungry; but, if diamonds are scarce, one can get on tolerably without them.

3. So, on the other hand, if there were to be a greatly increased supply of a perishable article, the price will fall more rapidly than in case of a more durable commodity. In the early autumn, there may be, in a market-town, two or three times as many peaches as are ordinarily consumed: as these will quickly decay, prices will go far below the natural value, since it will be better for the seller to get back even a part of their cost, than to have them perish on his hands. But if instead of peaches the commodity be cloth or iron or leather, the difference of price occasioned by an overstocked market is comparatively small. There are other cases of variation; but these illustrations are, perhaps, all that are necessary.

CHAPTER III.

THE PROMOTION OF COMMERCE.

1. WHATEVER tends to promote association conduces to human prosperity. Every obstruction to this is a damage. If men are kept apart so that they cannot combine, production will be scanty, and man, in the struggle with nature, will be at great disadvantage. Whatever brings men into such relations that all can minister freely to each, and each to all, furnishes increments of power. We have seen what are the conditions of high productiveness in a community, and that all these are in some way related to association. The same is true in the promotion of commerce.

2. Commerce will be promoted in general by such conditions as will render exchanges easy, frequent, and rapid. It is an advantage to the producer, to be able to dispose of his product as soon as possible after he has completed it. Whatever compels him to retain it on his hands for an indefinite period, or makes the opportunities of exchange remote and expensive, is detrimental to commerce and to all the interests it is designed to subserve. This is more obvious in the case of some commodities than in that of others. Many agricultural products must be sold within the year; others within a briefer period, or not at all. Certain garments and articles of personal decoration must also be sold within a moderate time after their manufacture, or they will become valueless through a change of the fashion.

The more readily a man can sell his own products, the more readily can he purchase those of others. Herein is implied that vigorous societary circulation which is characteristic of prosperous communities. Some of the particular conditions upon which this depends will now be set forth.

3. Commerce is promoted by the *close proximity of producer and consumer*. The first and most burdensome tax which the producer has to pay is that of *transportation*. This is more especially the case with the producer of raw material and of heavier and coarser commodities. It bears with particular weight upon the agriculturist. "If we estimate wheat at one dollar, and corn at fifty cents, a bushel, the value of the former will disappear, or become equal to zero, at two hundred and twenty miles, and the butter at a hundred and ten, if they must be conveyed by teams on common highways. Beyond those distances they will respectively become worthless for the purposes of sale, and the producer can have no pecuniary inducement to raise any larger quantity than suffices for his own consumption. The bulkier products — like potatoes, turnips, cabbages, etc. — become valueless at a still smaller distance. At twenty-five cents a bushel, potatoes cease to afford any remuneration to the grower fifty miles by common roads from markets, even if land were gratuitous, and the labor devoted to their cultivation could be procured for nothing."[1]

All so far said has reference to transportation by common roads. Every means by which this expense is diminished is a means of facilitating commerce. In the earlier periods of society, where there are no roads, and men have not even learned to avail themselves of beasts of burden, it is easy to see that there can be but little association, and the exchanges must be few. When these are brought into use,

[1] E. Peshine Smith, Manual of Political Economy, p. 196.

commerce will increase. When the iron railway supersedes the common road, and when resort is had to canals and water-courses, the obstacles are further diminished. But, under any system of transporting raw commodities great distances, their value is much less than if they were needed for consumption in the neighborhood. A bushel of corn raised in Nebraska will sell for a dollar in Massachusetts; but the producer must pay seventy-five cents to get it there. He may take his pay in cotton or woollen cloth, but he must pay something for their carriage; so that perhaps, counting the expense both ways, he scarcely realizes one-eighth as much for his product as if there were a Lowell or Manchester near by, instead of thirteen hundred miles distant. Cotton is raised in Alabama, and carried to England, four thousand miles away. Cloth is manufactured from this cotton, and carried back to Alabama. Now, the Alabama planter must sell his cotton for as much less than it will bring in England, as is required to pay not only the freight, but also insurance, brokers' commissions, and profits of merchants. He must pay a correspondingly additional price for his cloth. Some one has said, that, as it is cheaper to transport cloth than cotton, the planters would make a large saving if they would build factories in Alabama, convert the cotton into cloth, transport the cloth to England, and then bring it back to Alabama! It is impossible to estimate the diminution of expense when transportation is reduced to its lowest limits by bringing the several classes of producers into the closest possible proximity.

Nor is this all. There is a very large amount of both actual and possible product which cannot be exchanged at all when the producers are at remote distances from one another. We have already seen, that when local centres, in the form of manufacturing towns, are maintained in the midst of agricultural regions, there is, in addition to the great transportable staples, a vast variety of untransportable produce which finds a ready market. This requires comparatively little additional labor and capital. The value of it sometimes amounts to nearly as much in the aggregate as that of the main staples. There is thus not only a much greater productiveness, but a greater variety as well as larger facilities of exchange.

4. Closely connected with the advantage of the proximity of producer and consumer is that of *a large diversification of industries*. Indeed, in an important sense, the former depends upon the latter. It is only when one produces much of a single commodity, that one has the means to purchase many other commodities. As association or commerce depends on differences among individuals; the more numerous the differences, the more frequent and more extensive the exchanges. " In every community, the more numerous are the producers and the more various the productions, the more prompt, numerous, and extensive are the vents for those productions ; and, by a natural consequence, the more profitable are they to the producers, for prices rise with the demand. But this advantage is to be derived from real production alone, and not from forced circulation of products; for a value once created is not augmented in its passage from one hand to another." [1]

Just in proportion to the diversity of character and capability in a community, will that community approximate perfection ; for the perfection of society consists in the presence and combination, in proper proportions, of all the really different natural elements of humanity embodied in the various individual members, so that each will meet some want which another cannot supply. In a greatly heterogeneous

[1] Say's Political Economy, American edition, p. 81.

society, the development is greater, and there is a higher education, and more skill, invention, and enterprise, than in the opposite. Such a society will devise new industries peculiar to itself, and will thus furnish occasions for exchange with other communities, far more than would otherwise be the case.

There are two other topics which are intimately connected with the commercial prosperity of a community; but they are of such great importance and of so complicated a character, that they need to be discussed at considerable length. I refer to the questions of *free trade and protection*, and the subject of *finance*.

CHAPTER IV.

PROTECTION AND FREE TRADE.

1. A PROTECTIVE tariff, so called, is a system of duties levied by the government of a country on commodities produced in other countries, to prevent their coming into unequal competition with similar commodities of domestic production in such a way as to cripple or destroy the industry implied in the latter. Thus, suppose that iron may be manufactured in England, and delivered here at twenty dollars a ton; while, at the ordinary rate of profit and wages, iron could not at present be manufactured here for less than twenty-five dollars a ton. A duty of five dollars a ton is levied on the foreign iron. This enables our manufacturers to compete with those of England in our own market. It is claimed that in this way the home industry gets a chance to live, and become developed, and that such a development is an advantage to the country greater than the loss implied in the increase of price. We are not to consider here these duties in the light of a revenue to the government, though this they may be at the same time. But it is the *protective* feature only that we are to discuss; and, for that reason, it is desirable to abstract it from the revenue feature.

Free trade, as a theory, opposes all those duties the design of which is to afford any advantage to domestic industry.

It implies the same freedom of intercourse between producers in different nations as between those in the same community.

2. In an elementary treatise it is proper, that, on controverted questions, there should be a fair statement of the main arguments on both sides; though it is not necessary that the writer should conceal his own convictions.

The following are the principal positive arguments in favor of a restrictive system: —

1. It is said to be *the only sure defence of new and feeble industries against the unequal competition of those long established in other communities.* Freedom of competition is advocated by all parties. But it is denied that this exists in the cases above supposed. A community which has long experience, skilled labor, and accumulated capital, possesses advantages in the contest with a nation which is destitute of them. A restrictive system is the only method by which industries which have been for any reason wanting, especially in a new country, can be built up in competition with those of the same kind long established in another nation. Time, experience, and accumulated capitals give a superiority which must prove fatal to the industries which are wanting in these respects, unless resort be had to artificial measures to equalize the condition. This is admitted by J. S. Mill, the ablest as well as the most candid of recent free-trade writers. He says, "The superiority of one country over another, in a branch of production, often arises only from having begun it sooner. It cannot be expected that individuals should at their own risk, or rather to their certain loss, introduce a new manufacture, or bear the burden of carrying it on, until the producers have been educated up to the level of those with whom the processes have become traditional. A protective duty continued for a reasonable time will sometimes be the

least inconvenient mode in which a country can tax itself for the support of such an experiment." [1]

But, besides these natural advantages of an older and more experienced community, there is another of a purely artificial character, which is liable to be taken. Sometimes the manufacturers of one country adopt positive measures to break down the competing industries in feebler communities. To show that this is no chimera, the report of a British parliamentary committee, made about the year 1858, is sometimes cited. "The laboring classes generally, in the manufacturing districts of this country, are very little aware of the extent to which they are often indebted, for their being employed at all, to the immense *losses* which their employers voluntarily incur in bad times in order to destroy foreign competition, and to gain and keep possession of foreign markets. Authentic instances are well known of employers having in such times carried on their works at a loss amounting in the aggregate to three or four hundred thousand pounds in the course of three or four years. If the efforts of those who encourage the combination were to be successful for any length of time, the great accumulations of capital could no longer be made, which enable a few of the most wealthy capitalists to overwhelm all foreign competition in times of great depression, and thus clear the way for the *whole trade* to step in when prices revive, and to carry on a great business before *foreign* capital can again accumulate to such an extent as to be able to establish a competition in prices with any chance of success. The large capitals of this country are the great instruments of warfare (if the expression may be allowed) against the competing capital of foreign countries."

Said Lord Brougham in 1815 in Parliament, "England can afford to incur some loss on the export of English goods,

---

[1] Principles of Political Economy (American edition). vol. ii. pp. 538, 539.

for the purpose of destroying foreign manufactures in their cradle." Since such purposes are avowed, and since large capitals are used as "instruments of warfare" to break down foreign competing industries, there ought to be some defence against them. Such a defence, it is claimed, is found in a system of restrictive duties.

2. It is urged that *such a system gives a steady and uniform market* at an expense far less than the benefit accruing. Domestic commerce is liable to disturbances and revulsions through the free admission of commodities from the prolific industries of older countries. If the manufacturer be relieved from this unequal competition, he can keep his capital constantly employed, and, by reason of furnishing steady work, can secure better labor at less cost. Otherwise he may be compelled to stop work half of the time, and let his machinery lie idle, dismissing his laborers, to their great loss and distress. This is one reason why, as will hereafter be seen, it is claimed that manufactured products are often sold at lower prices under a protective tariff than when no duty is levied on the imported article. It is thought to be evident from these considerations, that certain desirable industries will spring up at once, and without appreciable extra expense, if they have *a fair chance*, which may nevertheless be prevented by unequal competition. They simply need to be shielded from the malign influence of parties interested to break them down, as well as from that of the natural inequality which exists between an infant industry and one that is fully developed.

3. It is urged in favor of protection, that it greatly aids the tendency to that *societary completeness* which is the final cause of *association*. The less obstructed the latter is, the more nearly perfect will the former become, and the stronger and more competent will men be. This freedom of asso-

ciation, as we have seen, depends upon the *individual differences* both of character and calling which prevail in a community. A variety of industries would be likely to grow up in any society left free to the development of its own resources. But a new society, whose nascent industries are in competition with those of an older and richer community, is *not* left free to develop its resources : the so-called freedom becomes a positive repression.

4. The restrictive system is regarded as *an advantage to the general interests of the community*, as well as to those particularly protected. If this were not the case, it would be altogether undeserving of support. We may take as a representative of these *agriculture*, since this is the fundamental industry, and, if the statement is true concerning this, it undoubtedly is of all others. In considering the protective system in relation to agriculture, several things are to be taken into account.

(1) First, there is the question of *transportation*. That every reasonable means should be taken to diminish the expense of this, no one doubts. It cannot be effected by doing or continuing to do the least immediately costly thing, but, frequently, only by going to much additional expense. This expense, however, is *once for all;* and so, on the whole, it is less expensive. To build a wagon-road where there was none before, involves an outlay sometimes of hundreds of thousands of dollars. It may add only a small amount the first year to the profit of each producer living near it; but in a brief period thereafter, the advantage will amount to much more than the whole cost of construction. The same principle applies in the building of railways and the making of canals.

If it is good economy to go to great expense to increase the power of association by means of roads and other transit arrangements, it certainly cannot be poor economy to go to some expense for the purpose, so far as the conditions allow, of doing away with transportation altogether. Restrictive duties, even when the conditions are the least favorable, are often the least expensive method by which the producer and the consumer can be brought into close proximity.

(2) Again, unless manufacturing centres exist in the midst of agricultural areas, products of the soil must be conveyed to a great distance. But *this implies virtually an exportation of the soil*, and this is a diminution of the capital of the farmer. There are many illustrations of this. Fifty years ago Western New York was one of the richest wheat-producing regions in the world: twenty-five years later it had so deteriorated that the crops were scarcely half their former amount. The wheat-fields of Ohio formerly yielded as high as thirty bushels to the acre: they afterwards fell off to fifteen and thirteen. The same process is going on in Illinois, Wisconsin, Iowa, and other purely agricultural regions. The soil is being rapidly exhausted, except where it is kept up by artificial fertilization. It has been said, that this might be done universally as well as in a few cases. But the fact that almost universally it is not done, would seem to indicate some natural reason for the failure.

On the other hand, agricultural estates within moderate distances from manufacturing centres tend to a constant increase of efficiency. "In England, in the days of the Plantagenets, when the population but little exceeded two millions, an acre of land yielded but six bushels of wheat; and, small as were the number to be fed, famines were frequent and severe. To-day we see eighteen millions occupying the same surface, and obtaining greatly increased supplies of very superior food." The yield of wheat now in England is thirty, forty, and even fifty bushels to the acre.

In France the product of grain has nearly doubled within a single century, while the population has increased only about fifty per cent. Here, as also in England, are new varieties of produce, which by themselves are equivalent to two-thirds of all the food formerly produced. There are still more striking illustrations found in Holland and Belgium, and in many other countries there are remarkable instances of a similar kind. This condition of things is possible only with a diversified industry out of which will come populous centres. This, in a new country, is conditioned on considerable expenditure, and such public measures as will prevent destructive foreign competition.

(3) A third advantage to agriculture is alleged to be found in *the utilization of materials which would otherwise be wasted.* In exclusively agricultural sections, an incalculable amount of produce, which might be furnished at scarcely any additional expense, is lost by reason of the difficulty or impossibility of transportation. It is only in the vicinity of manufacturing centres, that certain articles have any value at all. It was said some twenty-five years ago, that the crop of straw in France was utilized to the amount of a hundred and fifty million dollars a year. This is more than the value of our whole cotton-crop at that time, — a crop which employed the principal part of the capital and labor of ten States, and was the largest export by far of all our great staples. Yet, in large agricultural areas of our country, this material is every year burned in the fields where it grows.

5. A fifth argument advanced in favor of protection is, that *it tends to prevent the degradation of labor in the country protected.* It is generally urged, that one chief reason why in our own country manufactures are at a disadvantage in relation to those of European nations, is because the com-

pensation there is smaller than here. Even in England, where it is better than in most parts of the Continent, all the ruder kinds of labor are at a price which affords only such and so much sustenance as will keep the subject in a fair working condition. The great mass of this class is exceedingly poor, there are among them scarcely any savings, there is little inducement to them to endeavor to improve their condition, and there is very little hope to them of amelioration. Now, it is thought to be inevitable, that free reciprocal commerce with a country whose system produces such consequences can but result in reducing our own laboring population to nearly the same level. Two lakes lying near each other, but between which there is a channel of unrestricted communication, will stand at the same level.

CHAPTER V.

ARGUMENTS IN FAVOR OF FREE TRADE.

1. THE following are the main arguments in favor of free trade : —

1. It is said to be *the method of nature.* There is a great variety in the relative advantages possessed by different countries for the production of different commodities. " For instance, the mixture of coal and iron-stone in alternate seams gives England a striking advantage in the manufacture of hardware. On the other hand, a country like France has peculiar facilities for the growth of wheat : her land is fertile, and her labor is cheap. It may therefore be assumed, that in England iron is comparatively less costly to produce than wheat, and that in France the production of wheat is comparatively less costly than that of iron. In order to explain the advantage which each of these derives from trading with the other, let it be supposed that in France the production of a ton of pig-iron requires as much labor and capital as the production of twenty sacks of wheat ; but that in England the same quantity of iron requires as much labor and capital as would produce ten sacks of wheat ; then iron estimated in wheat is twice as valuable in France as in England. England, therefore, might say to France, 'It will be greatly to our mutual advantage if you will let me supply you with iron, and receive from you wheat in exchange for

it. For, suppose you give me fifteen sacks of wheat for each ton of iron, then we shall each gain five sacks of wheat on every transaction. If you manufacture the ton of iron yourself, it would cost you as much as twenty sacks of wheat; whereas you have only to give me fifteen sacks. On the other hand, I should only be able to get ten sacks of wheat for a ton of iron, if I sold the iron in my own country. We, therefore, each of us obtain a profit upon the transaction which is represented in value by five sacks of wheat. This is a great gain and saving of wealth, for the gain is made at no one's expense.'"[1]

2. Free trade is said *to conserve and increase the productive power of labor*, by causing it to be applied to those particular branches of industry for which each community has the greatest natural advantage. It is admitted by every one, that it would be a great waste to attempt the introduction of certain industries into places which furnish no natural facilities for them, and where no facilities can be created. To essay the cultivation of oranges in Minnesota, or cotton in Iowa, instead of raising wheat in both and exchanging it for the oranges and cotton, would be obviously preposterous. If it would be altogether unprofitable to undertake the cultivation of a new product where the facilities are wholly wanting, would it not be to some extent unprofitable where they are partly adverse? Hence all industries whose introduction depends upon artificial measures and considerable expense are regarded as so far forth uneconomical. If successful in their establishment, it is said, they can but divert labor and capital from those employments for which better conditions exist, and thus diminish the productive power of the community.

3. "*The right of property implies freedom for every one to do what he will with his own, provided he does not infringe*

[1] Henry Fawcett: Manual of Political Economy, pp. 372, 373.

on the rights of others." Any restriction of this freedom is *prima facie* a violation of a natural and inherent right. Every man is entitled to use the products of his own labor as may seem most for his advantage, to exchange them with citizens of his own country or with foreigners, as he may get for them the largest compensation. Any interference with this right bears the semblance of robbery.[1]

4. *"All obstruction to the exchange of commodities between any two countries desiring each other's products must injuriously affect the interests of both."* This is clearly seen in the case of natural obstacles. Mr. Amasa Walker makes use of the following illustration : " Two communities dwelling near each other are separated by a lofty chain of mountains, which renders transportation between them so difficult as to nearly preclude all intercourse. On one side of the mountain the soil is so admirably adapted to cereals that wheat (and other grains in proportion) can be produced at the rate of one bushel for a day's labor ; while fuel is so difficult to be obtained, that six days' labor are required to produce one ton of coal.

"On the opposite side of the mountain-range, so little is the soil adapted to the culture of grain that three days' labor are required to produce a single bushel of wheat ; while the facilities for mining coal are so great that one day's labor will purchase a ton. Under such circumstances, it would evidently be quite advantageous to both communities to exchange products, if there were no obstacles to prevent their doing so. Owing, however, to the resistance which the supposed mountains interpose, the transportation of a bushel of wheat is equivalent to two days' labor ; so that the wheat would cost three days' labor when brought to the coal country, and for that amount of labor the inhabitants could procure it

[1] Chapin's Wayland's Political Economy, p. 356.

themselves. So of the coal: to transport a ton which cost but one day's labor at the mines, would require the labor of five days; and therefore the people in the grain country, who can produce it by six days' work, would gain nothing by getting it from abroad. For these reasons, there would be no trade or exchange of products, so far as those articles were concerned, except in case of some accident, — as the failure of a crop, or an unexpected obstruction to the process of mining, by which the cost of the supposed commodity should be enhanced. Virtually there would be no profitable trade between the two communities, although in one coal was six times as dear, and in the other wheat was three times as dear, as in the neighboring country.

"If, however, we now suppose a railway to be made which reduces the *transportation* of a bushel of wheat to one day's labor, and the freight of a ton of coal to three days', we shall have conditions under which an advantageous trade will be sure to spring up: since the wheat-grower of the grain country can now get a ton of coal for the labor of four days, thus saving two days on each ton, equal to thirty-three and one-third per cent; and the coal-miner can get a bushel of wheat for two days' labor instead of three, thus saving, as far as his consumption of wheat is concerned, one-third, or thirty-three and one-third per cent, of his labor."[1]

That in such a case the removal of the obstruction, though at a very great cost, would result in far greater profit to both communities, has already been clearly shown in the chapter on the "Promotion of Commerce." It is claimed to follow from this, that, if the removal of obstructions to the freedom of commercial intercourse is beneficial, the creation of obstructions or restrictions, in whatever form, must be deleterious and damaging.

[1] Science of Wealth, pp. 94-96.

5. "*Free commercial intercourse between the nations of the earth tends evidently to establish their mutual relations upon a basis of peace and good-will.* By the mutual exchange of values, different peoples become acquainted with each other; and the feeling of interdependence creates a common interest, out of which grow the bonds of abiding friendship. Within the last two hundred years, international law has come to the dignity of a distinct science. Its development and growth have been coincident with the expansion of commerce under the improved facilities secured by recent inventions. The spontaneous and necessary intercourse of nations originates international law, and leads to the establishment of rules for governing that intercourse. The more the principles and rules of this department of law are studied, the more clearly does it appear, that, through free commercial relations, the separate interests of all nations are bound together in one, so that each is concerned in the welfare of every other, and each is induced to place itself in an attitude of friendship rather than of enmity towards others. Free trade, then, appears thus the promoter and pledge of peace in the world. The broad competition which it incites tends to swell the sum of human comforts and joys, and to impel every branch of the race to improve to the utmost the conditions of human living." [1]

2. Some of the strongest arguments in favor of free trade will, from the very nature of the case, be found in the form of *objections* to protection. Some of these I will briefly set forth.

1. Protective duties *violate the right of every man to do what he will with his own.* He has the natural right to buy where he can buy at the best advantage; and if the Government, by any kind of restriction, prevents his doing this, it

[1] Chapin's Wayland, p. 357.

goes beyond its authorized limits, and does him a positive injury.

2. Restrictive duties are *of the nature of a tax upon all the other industries, for the support of those protected.* This may be illustrated by the instance of the duty on iron. As was seen in the previous statement of the case, a duty of five dollars a ton on the foreign product would enable the American producer to compete with the foreign manufacturers. The objection claims that *all* iron — not only that imported, but that manufactured at home — is five dollars a ton higher in price by reason of this duty. That is, supposing that one hundred thousand tons are imported: the duties paid to the Government amount to five hundred thousand dollars. But suppose there are also three hundred thousand tons made here: this being also five dollars a ton higher than without restriction, the aggregate additional amount paid will be fifteen hundred thousand dollars, none of which goes to the Government as revenue, but all to the manufacturers as bonus; and all of it must be contributed by the users of iron.

3. It is objected further to the restrictive system, that *it causes a diminution of exports* from the country adopting it. The argument is, in brief, that, by restricting the imports, the country loses the opportunity of selling to foreign producers, since they must pay for commodities purchased of the former with goods of their own; and, if their goods are not taken, they cannot purchase others.

4. It is also objected, that, while the system is advocated as a protection to infant industries, these *never come to maturity*. It is said that some industries that have been thus fostered for thirty, forty, or fifty years, are still as clamorous as ever for protection, and that they are no nearer going alone now than at the beginning.

5. The question is asked, "If restriction is good as between different nations, why is it not good between different communities of the same nation?" The United States is cited as a magnificent example of free trade over a large part of a continent, and of the prosperity and development which is consequent upon such a system.

6. The last objection to be mentioned is, that it gives *monopoly privileges*. By this evidently is meant that it gives advantages to a few, which are denied to the many. The protected industries are supposed to be favored, as has before been seen, at the expense of those not protected.

3. It has been the design to present the arguments on both sides, as clearly and forcibly as possible with the limits at our disposal. Some of the arguments on both sides are specious rather than conclusive; though, of course, different writers see in them severally different degrees of force. It is not improbable that much more stress has been laid upon the protectionist argument of the prevention of the degradation of labor, than belongs to it. While labor is better paid generally in the United States than in almost any other country, it is not therefore necessarily any more costly to the employer; since the costliness of labor is estimated not so much by the amount paid for it as by its greater or less efficiency. We have already seen, that, while in England wages are higher than on the Continent, the same *effect* of labor costs less in the former than in the latter. So if we compare the European Continent with Southern Asia. Doubtless the same comparison will furnish analogous results as between this country and Great Britain. Still, if it be true that the unequal competition which would result under free trade prevents the development of industries for which a community has good facilities, the growth of capital would thus be hindered, and labor would be at a growing disadvantage.

4. On the other hand, there is some force in the objection to protection, that the success of free trade, as applied to the different parts of a great country like the United States, would seem to indicate the propriety of applying it to the different communities of the world. There is, however, this difference, — that this country is, in an important sense, one community, having a common financial system, a common system of domestic commerce, and many other interests in common. For this reason it might seem that the policy demanded here is widely different from that applicable to nations in their mutual relations.

5. These are two or three of the arguments against and objections to protection, that seem fallacious. The reason given in favor of free trade, that it is *the method of nature*, is one of these. The theory is certainly very simple and natural. But it is said, simplicity and naturalness, if these terms imply the exclusion of art, do not by any means indicate superiority. If they do, we must give the preference to barbarism over civilization. All improvement and development involve the application of art and artificial methods. It is no argument against a system, that it is partly artificial instead of exclusively natural; provided only that art shall work with nature, and not against it. In actual life, no one thinks of leaving nature to create industries or remove obstructions. We have a good illustration of this in the fifth argument for free trade. Mr. Walker there supposes the case of two communities of diverse productive capabilities, but separated by a range of mountains which rendered commerce impracticable. He has no hesitation in approving the building of a railroad to remedy this difficulty. He does not for a moment think of waiting for *nature* to do it, but would resort to art, and incur great expense, in order to bring the two kinds of producers into close proximity.

6. One of the most popular and effective objections to protection is, that it is of the nature of a tax on other industries. Yet it seems to me to be specious and fallacious. The assumption is, that the consumer pays for the protected article a price equivalent to that which it would be if there were no duty, plus the duty. As a matter of fact, there are very few instances in which this is really the case. It is true, that, in many instances, the price of a protected article will rise, and for a time continue higher, because of the duty imposed. The idea of protection implies this : it is a sacrifice made in the present, for the sake of future advantage. Yet there are instances in great numbers where the price, instead of increasing, diminishes on the imposition of a protective duty. Nor is this any thing abnormal, but perfectly in accordance with economical laws, as we shall see in a few illustrative examples.

"Years ago," says Mr. Greeley, "under a low duty, we imported most of the starch used in this country, making a little capriciously when the market, from whatever cause, was bare ; but soon a fresh importation would flood our ports, shutting up our starch-factories, and driving our workmen to find employment at something else. Of course they acquired no proficiency in the art, and our starch was undoubtedly inferior in quality to its imported rival. But the tariff of 1842 imposed a duty of two cents a pound on imported starch ; and at once a leading house in this city [New York] resumed its long-suspended manufacture of starch, called in its scattered workmen, made a good article, and put it on the market half a cent per pound below the price previously ruling. This was done on purely business principles, because starch could be afforded for less in a large and steady market than in one contracted and capricious."

The same effect was seen in the case of cotton fabrics.

The increased duties amounted to nearly one hundred per cent on importers' prices; and, according to the theory of the objection under consideration, it should have nearly doubled the price. But instead of this, the prices in the Lowell manufacturers' lists were lower by from one-fourth of a cent to a cent and a half per yard. It was for the same reason as that adduced in the case of the starch, — a steady and uniform market, occasioned by a restrictive duty, enabled the manufacturers to produce cheaper than with the contrary conditions.

The history of the Bessemer steel-rail manufacture in this country is another notable example. In 1864, there was no manufactory of this kind in this country: all the steel rails used were imported from England, and sold at a hundred and fifty dollars per ton in gold. There was a duty of forty-five per cent *ad valorem*. Certain parties interested in extending the use of these rails on our roads went to England to negotiate for the purchase of a quantity of them, but could make no more favorable terms than those above mentioned. Upon their return, a company was organized, works involving great expense were constructed, and workmen were imported. All this time the English rails were selling at $150 to $162. But the American product was put at $130, when instantly the English article was offered at the same price, and, soon after, at $120. Two years later, when the increase of the manufacture threatened to drive out the foreign article, the price of English rails was put at $110, and, soon after, at $80. This was below the cost of production to our manufacturers, and their mills were in danger of being closed at an enormous loss of capital. At this point, fifteen of the *consumers* of steel rails petitioned Congress to increase the duty. Attention is called to the fact that these petitioners were consumers, persons interested in a diminution, and not in an increase, of prices; and it was in this interest that they petitioned. They knew, that, if this competition were destroyed, prices would again rise exorbitantly. The request was granted, though only to the extent of about four per cent, but enough to secure the American enterprise from being overborne. Under the stimulus of this action, there has been an extraordinary development of the manufacture; and the prices have constantly tended downward, till now steel rails are sold for about thirty-five dollars a ton.

If it be said that much of this diminution comes from the improvements in methods of manufacture, this may be freely admitted; and yet it is tolerably evident that a very large proportion of these improvements came from the establishment of the manufacture in America, and the sharp competion occasioned thereby. It is also clearly evident that no such improvements took place, within two or three years, as to reduce the price from a hundred and sixty-two dollars to a hundred and five dollars.

The same phenomena, though less marked, are found in connection with the protected manufactures of silk, of worsted, and many others, where prices have steadily declined, and almost in a ratio with the increase of the industry here. It is useless to say, that, in so many cases, this diminution is owing wholly to other causes. So many instances, and under such varied circumstances, would seem positively to indicate some common cause.

7. The objection that protection *causes a decrease of exports* is largely insisted on by many writers; but there are many others who deny that it has any force. In the first place, it is said, if it were true that the protected country had no need of the goods from abroad, by reason of manufacturing them at home, it would also have no need to send

its own products abroad; since there would be, by the very fact before mentioned, all the larger demand for them at home. It is not necessary to import simply for the sake of importing, nor to export for the sake of exporting. But in the second place it must be admitted, that, after each nation has exhausted all its own facilities of production, there will still be many desirable things, which, if had at all, must be imported. It is also true again, that those communities which most largely and judiciously multiply their own industries, and thereby cultivate societary completeness, are the communities which have the largest variety of productions peculiar to themselves, and liable to be wanted by other communities. Hence it is that those nations which have the greatest diversity of industries are those whose foreign trade is also the largest. It is in accordance with this principle, that we find, that, in the nations in which the protective policy prevails, the foreign trade, instead of diminishing as the objection assumes, increases more than in the unprotected, or slightly protected, countries. Take the United States as an example. In the decade from 1870 to 1880, under a tariff exceptionally high, and having many other exceptional features,—a tariff under which, if under any that was possible, the unfavorable effect under consideration should have been conspicuous,—we find that the exports increased from $420,500,275 in value, to $841,501,388, or a little more than a hundred per cent; and the imports, from $376,616,473 in value, to $741,501,725, or a little less than a hundred per cent.

Take the case of France. More than fifty years ago, the "Edinburgh Review," in an article on French industry and commerce, predicted, that, under the protective system then in operation there, the foreign trade of that country would be nearly ruined. During the decade in the middle of which this prediction was made, the exports of France averaged but little more than 500,000,000 francs. In 1854, about twenty-five years later, they amounted to 1,400,000,000 francs, having nearly trebled. In 1874, France having then recently greatly increased her protective duties after a period of relaxation, her exports to Great Britain and Ireland alone amounted to 1,907,212,655 francs; being nearly three times the value of the British exports to France.

8. It is undoubtedly the fact, that the protective system has been often perverted from its legitimate purposes, and that any tariff arranged with reference to this principle will operate with great inequality. This is also the case with every system of taxation. Still, in view of the arguments on both sides briefly presented, it seems apparent, that, to such a nation as our own especially, far more good than evil would come from a judicious application of the principle of restriction. That our present system is greatly imperfect, and that in many instances it is excessive, is not at all unlikely. But that the country would find advantage in the entire abandonment of the system, is vastly improbable.

CHAPTER VI.

THE INSTRUMENT OF EXCHANGE.

1. WHATEVER aids in increasing the facilities of association, enhances the power of man over nature. The necessity of *money* as such a means is easily made manifest. The design of commerce is, that each person, while producing but a single commodity, or, at most, but a very few commodities, may equitably avail himself of the many commodities that he needs. We have seen, that, though one man may produce but one thing, he may produce enough of this to supply a thousand persons. At the same time he may need a thousand things which he does not produce. Hence a thousand men find opportunity to minister to his support.

2. The first exchanges in primitive times would naturally be by barter, each one exchanging the surplus of his own products for such surplus of others as he himself might desire. But the necessity of some other method would early evince itself. It would be found to be inconvenient and expensive for the shoemaker who has made a dozen pair of shoes, to go with them to all the other producers whose wares he may just at that time particularly want. Even if the expense could be in some way mitigated, there would be still other serious embarrassments. He might want a hat, but perhaps the hatter does not at that time want any shoes. He desires a coat; but the tailor may only want a single pair of shoes, while an equal exchange would require six or seven pairs. Thus, to find purchasers of his own commodity among those whose commodities he desires in quantities corresponding to those of his desired by them, would be a protracted and tedious business.

A partial remedy for this inconvenience would be found in the agency of *trade*, — the establishment of places where all kinds of commodities would be taken by the merchant, and where within certain limits one would be reasonably sure to find whatever was desirable in return for products brought in. This might be further supplemented by book-account. But, greatly as these devices would abridge and expedite the business of exchange, it would be found that not only an *agency* is necessary, but also an *instrument*, — a medium readily receivable for all commodities, and in exchange for which all desirable commodities would be readily taken.

CHAPTER VII.

THE PRECIOUS METALS.

1. The great majority of political economists agree as to certain characteristics which should belong to any substances used as the medium of exchange. The mere enumeration of these indicates the reason why certain metals have been almost universally accepted for this purpose. 1. It is said that the material should have value, aside from its use as money. 2. It should be generally uniform in value ; that is, the value should not be greater in one place than in another. 3. It should comprise much value in small bulk. 4. It should have some close approximation to constancy of value. 5. It should not be easily destructible. 6. It should be divisible into small portions, which can be re-united without loss. 7. It must be of universal use. 8. It must be capable of receiving and retaining stamps and marks indicating its current value.

These characteristics are attributed to gold and silver. 1. They have a natural value, aside from that implied in their use as money. They are employed in the arts, though to a less extent than for the purpose of money. On this account, should either of them be demonetized to any considerable extent, the value would greatly diminish. 2. Being simple substances, and, in proportion to their value, easily transportable, it has been generally held that they were of the same value in every part of the world. This, however, is denied by several eminent writers. It is not practicable to fully discuss this question, but I will refer to an authority or two. Professor Cairnes, one of the ablest of recent writers on political economy, in speaking of the doctrine that the value of gold is the same all the world over, says, " Now, if this be so, as the value of gold is merely another expression for the gold prices of commodities, it must follow that a high or low scale of general prices existing in any country, and not shared by every other, is an impossible occurrence. As there is no local value of gold, there can be no local scale of prices. I have no hesitation, however, in expressing my opinion that the doctrine in question, with whatever confidence advanced, is totally destitute of foundation."[1] Ricardo had some time before said, " The value of money is never the same in any two countries; depending, as it does, on relative taxation, on manufacturing skill, the advantages of climate, natural productions, and many other causes." Other writers, while substantially admitting the truth of the above statements, claim that the variation is not of large amount. Yet obviously it must vary with the scale of general prices.

3. That these substances comprise much value in small bulk, is sufficiently palpable. 4. It has also been generally held, that gold and silver are constant and uniform in their value. Yet it has of late been evident, that, with the vastly increased production of these metals, their value has greatly diminished : but this diminution, it is claimed, comes gradually and through the lapse of years; so that the change is scarcely appreciable within the time for which contracts are ordinarily made. Most writers regard them as far less variable than any other commodity which at present exists. It

[1] Leading Principles of Political Economy, etc., p. 408.

is highly probable, however, that far too great an estimate has been placed upon this supposed characteristic. It comes in part from the confusion of price with value. The price of all other things is their value expressed in money. The price of money is its value expressed in itself. In other words, there is no such thing as *the price of money*. Where gold and silver are the basis of money, *they* have no price. But their *value*, like the value of other things, is their purchasing power. Because they are made a standard of value, and because this value is always equal to itself, we are easily deluded into the belief that it never varies.

Says M. Bastiat, an eminent economist of France, "A measure of length, size, and surface is a quantity agreed upon and unchangeable. It is not so with the value of gold and silver. This varies as much as that of corn, wine, cloth, and labor, and from the same causes; for it has the same source, and obeys the same laws. Gold is brought within our reach, just like iron, by the labor of miners, the advances of capitalists, and the combination of merchants and seamen. It costs more or less, according to the expense of its production, according to whether there is little or much in the market, whether it is little or much in request; in a word, whether it undergoes the fluctuations of all other human productions."[1] Professor Fawcett holds that "The value of gold accurately varies in the inverse ratio of the prices of commodities. If the prices of all commodities rise one hundred per cent, the value of gold falls one hundred per cent; for the same quantity of gold will exchange for, or purchase, only one-half as much of the commodity."[2]

---

[1] Essays in Political Economy (Putnam's translation), p. 166.

[2] Manual of Political Economy, pp. 365, 366. There is a singular error in this statement, which it seems strange that such a writer should make. If prices rise one hundred per cent, gold falls *fifty* per cent. If it should fall one hundred per cent, its value would be nothing at all.

5. These metals are among the most indestructible of substances, and the wear and tear of them is inconsiderable and inexpensive.

6. They are divisible into small portions, to suit the convenience of users; and can be readily re-united by melting, whenever desirable. In this respect they differ from diamonds, which comprise even greater value in the same small bulk; but when the latter have been once divided into fragments, they cannot be re-united. Another difference is, that gold and silver have a value proportional to their quantity; while, in the case of diamonds, the larger are usually of proportionally greater value, — that is, a diamond twice as large as another may be of five times the value.

7. Gold and silver are also of almost universal use, and can be transported from one country to another at slight expense.

8. Finally, they are capable of receiving stamps and marks in the way of coinage, by which their character and value are indicated.

2. These characteristics of gold and silver have made them media of exchange from very early ages, even before men were fixed in permanent habitations.

When and where coinage began, is not known; but probably it was somewhere in Western Asia, about 800 B.C. Though gold and silver are the most widely adopted media of exchange, they are not the only substances which have been used for this purpose: iron, cattle, wheat, tobacco, shells, beads, the skins of animals, and other articles, have officiated in this capacity.

3. The relation of government to money is a matter of some importance. It is to be observed, that gold and silver became the recognized instrument of exchange in the early civilizations, not by any arbitrary edict of rulers, but by the

spontaneous consent of society, growing out of a general perception of their natural fitness for this office. But it by no means follows that government has nothing to do in relation to it. Government must, for one thing, determine what shall be a *legal tender;* that is, what, when offered in payment of a debt, shall be a legal discharge of that debt. A vital object of legislation is, to prevent uncertainty in the interpretation of contracts. Accordingly, it must prescribe what shall constitute the fulfilment of a contract, or a discharge of its obligation. Otherwise there might be contention and costly litigation. Thus, one man owing another for a barrel of flour, the former might offer to pay in oats, of which the latter is not just now in want; or in glass bottles, which he will never want. Or the creditor might refuse to receive money of any kind, and demand some commodity difficult or impossible for the debtor to obtain. Government may prevent all liability to this trouble by determining, in cases where no commodity is designated, what shall be regarded as a fulfilment of the contract. But it will, at the same time, leave the contracting parties free to designate any material as the medium of payment; and, when so designated, both parties will be held to the terms of the agreement.

Government has also a function to exercise in determining the kinds of coins, their names, their weight, and the degree of purity of the metal; what shall be the monetary unit, and the stamps and marks to be put upon the several pieces to distinguish them. It may also punish any corruption or counterfeiting of the coin. It must fix the monetary standard, and determine whether it shall be one or the other, or both, or neither, of the precious metals. These have been regarded by most writers as the main functions of the government in relation to money; and it has generally been taught, that much beyond these it is not possible for the government to go without transcending its sphere.

4. What shall constitute the monetary standard? is a question open to some discussion. Three different standards have been in use in different modern nations, and at different times. Some have fixed upon gold, others upon silver, and others still upon both. As between gold and silver, the preference depends chiefly upon the stability of their respective values, but subordinately also upon the convenience of handling. There is not only a difference among the several nations concerning the standard adopted, but the same nation has changed its standard, and sometimes more than once. Many years ago, Germany adopted silver: within the last few years it has changed to gold. In 1858, Holland adopted silver, having previously had the double standard. She also has recently changed to the gold standard. What is called the Latin Monetary Union — comprising France, Belgium, Switzerland, Italy, and Spain — nominally adheres to the double standard, though the coinage of silver in all of them has been restricted, and for a time prohibited. Greece and Roumania have the same system, as do also Peru, Ecuador, and New Granada, in America. The single silver standard is maintained by Austria and Russia, though in these countries specie payment has been for a long time suspended. Nearly all the vast population of Asia make silver the legal standard, as do several nations on the American continent, — about one-third of the inhabitants of the world altogether.

Great Britain adopted the gold standard about sixty-seven years ago, — the first nation ever making the experiment. The same standard now exists in Portugal, Egypt, Turkey, the Scandinavian kingdom, a portion of South America, and the English colonies of Australasia and South Africa. Germany adopted gold about 1870, and the United States in 1873; but the latter returned to the double standard in 1878. In all these countries, silver is used as a subsidiary coin, and is made a legal tender for a limited amount.

5. The relative value of gold and silver varies from time to time. From the earliest period of which we have any record, — that is, from about 1600 B.C., — down to the beginning of the Christian era, they stood to one another in the relation of about 1 to 12 or 13, occasionally going up to 1 to 14, and once falling as low as 1 to 8.93. From that time to 1640 A.D., the ratio varied from 1 to 14.40 to 1 to 10.50. Since 1640 it has never gone below 1 to 14, nor so high as 1 to 16 till 1872. The legal ratio adopted by the European governments for many years has been that of 1 to $15\frac{1}{2}$. Since 1872, there have been marked variations in the ratio. For a while it increased greatly, at one time going as high as 1 to 22.54, though this was temporary. For most of the time it has been 1 to 17 or 18.

CHAPTER VIII.

CERTAIN DOCTRINES CONCERNING MONEY CONSIDERED.

1. THAT money is not synonymous with wealth, is a proposition requiring little discussion. At this day, to most thoughtful persons, it appears like a truism. Yet, because in former times many wise men thought differently, and because some popular fallacies have grown out of the opposite doctrine, and are still extant, it is proper to give some attention to it. Some nations were so thoroughly imbued with this latter notion, that it became an important object of legislation, how to prevent any exportation of the precious metals; such exportation being regarded as so much subtracted from the wealth of the country. The world has been some ages in learning that wealth consists not in money, — which is only an instrument for the exchange of those articles constituting wealth, — but in the abundance of those things which command money.

2. The value of the money in circulation in the community need be only a small fraction of the value of the commodities exchanged through its instrumentality. To most thoughtful persons, this will appear also as a truism. Yet we sometimes hear men reasoning as though the value of the exchanges made were somehow equivalent to that of the money used in making them. A familiar example will illustrate the fact that a small sum of money will effect exchanges

involving many times its value. Suppose you are in want of a hat: you have five dollars, which you exchange with the hat-merchant for the article desired. The hatter pays it to a man of whom he has bought some wood. The latter buys with it a barrel of flour; and the flour-merchant gives it to one of his clerks, in payment for services. The clerk pays it for board to his landlady; and she puts it with other money, to discharge her quarter's rent-bill. The landlord sends it to his son at school, who uses it to pay his tuition. Here are exchanges to the amount of thirty-five dollars, though but one-seventh of that amount of money has been used. Thus it is evident that the money requisite to effect the exchanges of a community equals in value only that of a small part of the commodities exchanged through its use. As we shall see hereafter, the exchanges made without the direct intervention of money are still greater in proportion to the amount of the medium in circulation.

3. It is a commonly received doctrine, that the value of money is proportionally greater when its quantity is less, and *vice versa*. There is no doubt, that, as a general principle, this is true; yet the proposition is not to be construed too rigidly, and it is practically subject to many modifications. There is very little doubt, that, in a state of society otherwise perfectly stationary, where previously there had been *just the proper amount of money* to furnish the best facilities for exchange; where money was the sole instrument of exchange, and there was no resort to the mechanism of credit-transfers, — the introduction of a considerable addition to the amount of money in circulation would increase prices, while a subtraction from this amount would diminish prices.

The relation of the amount of money to general prices is affected by a variety of actual facts, some of which are pretty certain to be present in any state of civilized society.

1. There is seldom just the amount of money in circulation that would furnish the most nearly perfect facility of exchange. It is impossible to determine how much is needed in any given case. But it is certain that some particular quantity meets the conditions better than any other. If there be either more or less than this, commerce will be unfavorably affected. It is the doctrine of a certain school, that, if a purely metallic currency exist, "any amount is enough;" since, it is said, prices will adjust themselves to that amount. A distinguished statesman illustrates this by saying, that, if a single yardstick can measure one piece of cloth, it can measure any number of other pieces. This is true; but who would ever think of saying, that in a great dry-goods store, employing several scores of salesmen, "any number of yardsticks would be enough," since the business would adjust itself to the number? Evidently the number must be something more than a very few, or the business must suffer. If money is the instrument of exchange, there must be a certain ratio of the amount of money to the amount of exchange which is normal; and any variation from this can but be in some degree disadvantageous.

Suppose, that, in a nation where the amount of the circulating medium has been less than this normal quantity, by some means there is an increase. Now, no doubt, prices will rise. This will follow not merely because there is more money, but for other reasons as well. By the very hypothesis of there being too little previously, commerce was crippled, production was checked, labor was not fully or remuneratively employed; and the purchasing-power of the whole community was thus diminished, making the demand even smaller than the supply. The addition to the machinery of exchange would furnish a remedy for the depression: industries would revive, labor would be in demand, exchanges would be ready and quick, the purchasing-power of the community would be enhanced, and prices would rise. They would rise even without any addition to the stock of money, if, without this, these other conditions could have been secured. So that the increase of money causes the increase of prices, not merely by its own occurrence, but quite as much by the impulse its presence has given to business. We should find an equally clear illustration of the general principle in the case of a withdrawal of a portion of the circulating medium.

2. Another factor to be regarded here is that of the perpetually increasing facilities of production. These diminish the cost of commodities, and consequently cause prices to fall. The multiplication of the appliances by which the forces of nature are now compelled to do the work formerly performed slowly and painfully by man, is patent to the commonest observation. This very multiplication of production in proportion to cost would, of itself, tend to multiply exchange, and, so far forth, would create a greater demand for money to facilitate the exchanges; while, at the same time, the diminution of the cost of production would tend to depress prices. Hence, even if, other things being equal, the increase of money would enhance prices, the fact alluded to would wholly, and probably much more than, neutralize the effect.

There is yet another modifying fact to be noticed. The influence of the increase of productive facilities is felt much more in manufactured articles and finished commodities than in coarse products and raw material; so that while the former, under conditions usually existing in civilized communities, are continually growing cheaper, most agricultural and mining products, as also land and labor, tend to grow dearer. It is thus, as Mr. Carey has shown, that, in a prosperous community, the prices of raw material and of finished products more and more approximate.

3. It is evident that commerce, or at least the desire to exchange in our modern communities, tends to increase more rapidly than metallic money. Hence the various devices by which the various forms of credit are made to furnish a large supplementary mechanism of exchange, — by means of book-account, bank-deposits, bills of exchange, drafts, checks, etc. As we shall see hereafter, much the larger proportion of the world's exchanges are effected in this way. These methods would be adopted to some extent, even if the abundance of coin were ever so great. But there are limits to their profitable employment, and those limits are more likely to be overstepped when the supply of currency is scanty than when it is abundant.

It will be seen, from the foregoing considerations, that while money, like other objects of value, is subject to the law of supply and demand; and while, all other conditions remaining the same, prices are inversely as the amount of money, — yet there are so many and such complicated counter influences at work, that the rule is not only of little practical consequence, but it is sometimes false and misleading. Says Stephen Colwell, " The notion long prevalent, that prices were exactly adjusted to the quantity of currency, is shown to have long since exploded. Among the innumerable influences which go to determine the general range and fluctuation of prices, the quantity of money is found to be one of the least effective." [1]

[1] Ways and Means of Payment, p. 17.

CHAPTER IX.

THE CREDIT ELEMENT IN THE INSTRUMENT OF EXCHANGE.

1. So far, the only money spoken of, except incidentally, has been gold and silver. The characteristics which have made them the almost universal media of exchange have been indicated. Yet it must be evident to the most superficial observer, that, especially in recent times, they have constituted only a minor portion of the machinery of exchange. The chief reason for this is their limited quantity. Moreover, the amount of them which would now be absorbed in making *all* the exchanges of the commercial world, would render them too costly an instrument.

It is true that the production of these metals within the last few centuries, and especially within the last thirty-five years, has been very great. But great as has been the increase, the increase of demand for them would have been still greater but for the substitution of other devices. Besides the costliness of the material, even were there a sufficiency of it, the handling and conveyance of such vast sums as would at times be necessary, would be exceedingly inconvenient and expensive, if not at times impossible.

2. The system of credit would easily suggest itself, not only as a matter of convenience in other respects, but also as an instrument of exchange. Let us take the following as an illustration. In a rural region, a farmer buys of the country merchant from time to time, for a series of months, whatever he may need for his family or his farm, — small groceries, cotton cloth, crockery, furniture, scythes, rakes, hoes, shovels, etc.; with which he is duly debited. From time to time also he carries to the store, butter, eggs, cheese, apples, potatoes, wool, wheat, corn, etc.; with these he is credited. At the end of the year the accounts are balanced, and whatever difference there is — and ordinarily it would be small — might be paid in cash, or carried over to a new account. Thus exchange to the amount of several hundred dollars may be made, and only ten or fifteen dollars in money be used. Credit here in the form of *book-account* has been the instrument of exchange. It is to be noted, however, that reference is had, in all these exchanges, to money as the measure of values. The pound of tea is debited, not as so much tea, but as one dollar; the scythe and snath, not as such merely, but as three or four dollars, as the case may be. So the farmer is credited, not with the ten pounds of butter simply, but with three dollars; and the thirty pounds of cheese is put down as five dollars.

Now, let us suppose that the farmer, whom we will call A, has a balance of fifteen dollars in his favor in his settlement with the merchant, whom we may call B. A also settles with the blacksmith, whom we may designate as C, with whom he has an account of a similar character to that with B. Let us suppose that the balance here amounts to fifteen dollars against A. The latter may now give C an order on B for this amount. C takes it to B, who accepts it, and debits the amount to A. Possibly C may also have an account with B, and the balance against the former may be just fifteen dollars. In that case the amount debited to A on the acceptance of his order will be debited to C; and thus all three accounts, amounting perhaps to several hundred dollars, will be settled, and all balances paid, without the use of any money. This is called a *transfer of credit*, and, as we shall see hereafter, is a very large element in the mechanism of exchange. The above is a very simple instance, and yet contains all that is essential to a system which is variously implicated, and extends to transactions involving the value of many millions of dollars.

3. The following definition of credit is given by McCulloch: "Credit is the trust or confidence placed by one individual in another when he assigns him money or other property in loan, or without stipulating for immediate payment. The party who lends is said to give credit; the party who borrows, to obtain credit." The importance of credit, both as an instrument of exchange and as an aid to production, is very great. In order to production, as we have seen, a man must be able and willing to work, and there must be capital with which in some way he can unite his labor. The constituents of capital he must in very many instances borrow of some capitalist before he can work to any advantage in producing means of his own to exchange for the capital needed.

4. The advantages of credit may be briefly presented as follows: —

1. *To the capitalist.*

(*a*) Without a credit-system, each capitalist must keep all his means in his own hands, and thus incur the liability to extend his business beyond his ability to manage it. The limits of executive talent vary greatly in various men. Some can conduct the most extensive and complicated enterprises, involving perhaps millions of capital. Some, while able to earn fair or even large wages by their labor and skill, are yet incompetent to carry on even a small business of a simple character. Between these two extremes lie all the grades of business ability. Hence there will always be men with more capital than they can manage, while others will be competent to manage more capital than they own. It will, then, be for the interest of the former to become the creditors of the latter, if they can do so with good security.

(*b*) Again, there are those who have considerable incomes, the surplus of which, above their expenditures, it is impossible to invest in their own business. Lawyers, physicians, literary men, teachers, artists, and many others are included in this class. Widows and children are often left with property sufficient for their support, if it can be properly invested; but they cannot usually carry on business themselves. If their property can be safely loaned, both they and the community will find advantage in such a disposition of it.

(*c*) Finally, as men advance in years, they are less capable of superintending an extensive business. It is natural that there should be a contraction, rather than an expansion, of their enterprises. In some cases it is necessary for them to altogether retire. In either case it would involve the withdrawal of a part or a whole of their capital, which must lie idle or be loaned.

2. *To the non-capitalist.*

(*a*) A man works with more interest, vigor, and success, where the enterprise is his own, than where it belongs to another. Then, too, he can adapt himself to his work as to time and circumstances, as he could not were he a mere journeyman. He will thus be likely to greatly enhance his production, both in quantity and quality.

(*b*) Moreover, as we have seen, there are some men who have peculiar abilities of a high order for organization and management; which abilities, without borrowed capital, can find no good opportunity for exercise, and will thus be lost both to their possessors and to the community.

(*c*) If each retains his own property as capital, there will be accumulations in a few hands and places; whereas, with a wise credit-system, capital will be diffused more widely, and will bring the producer and consumer, as the capitalist and the laborer, into easier relations to each other.

5. It thus clearly appears, that, by a judicious system of credit, the capital of a community gets more fully combined with labor, and production is palpably increased. It is to be recollected, that what is ostensibly borrowed and lent is *money*, but really it is *material* and *implements*. Thus a man desires to set up in the business of a blacksmith. He has simply the ability to labor, and the skill and intelligence, that fit him for his vocation. But he has no shop, no tools, no coal, no iron. If some one would lend him these, with the understanding that he might pay for them under stipulated conditions, and thus become their owner, it would answer all his purposes. Possibly in some cases this would be done; but generally he would borrow the *money* with which to purchase these.

These are only some of the forms and advantages of credit. It must exist to a greater or less extent in nearly all transactions of men with men. The employer must either trust his workmen with pay in advance, or they must trust him till the work is done. In countless ways it ramifies through society, and aids in all the affairs of commerce as well as in the production of wealth. Without it, society could scarcely advance beyond the condition of barbarism. It is the essential element in all the great enterprises characterized by the combination and division of labor. In commerce, as in religion, "we walk by faith, not by sight." But we have to do with it here chiefly as supplementing the precious metals in the function of an instrument of exchange. As we shall see, credit, in one form and another, constitutes the larger part of this instrument.

CHAPTER X.

BANKS AND BANKING.

1. BANKS are institutions which serve to abbreviate and facilitate the business of exchange, by extending and rendering available the credit of the community. Of general banking business in ancient times, we have only meagre accounts. It is more than probable that something answering to our present system existed in several nations previous to the Christian era. In modern times, among the earliest financial institutions of which we have any account, were the banks of Venice and Genoa, chartered, the former in the twelfth and the latter in the fourteenth century, and continuing in operation till the beginning of the present century. The banks of Amsterdam and Hamburg began somewhat later, and are still in existence, having had a vast influence in the financial history of Europe. The Bank of England was created about 1692, and has been for more than a hundred years the most powerful factor in the commercial world. All of these institutions have been closely related to the governments of their respective countries. A multitude of minor banks have sprung up within the last two centuries, some of them of scarcely less note than those just mentioned. Banking is one of the most important occupations of our modern civilization.

2. The beginning of the modern system was probably

something in this way: In communities where there was a considerable variety of industry, and there were consequently many exchanges, there would necessarily be greater or smaller accumulations of money in the hands of individuals. It would be found inconvenient, hazardous, or expensive to keep these in one's own possession. A strong-box, perpetual watching, and manifold precautions might secure safety. But it would naturally occur to practical business men, that one strongly protected place, under the care of a competent person who should devote himself to the charge of the treasures of his employers, would be, at least, less expensive than each individual's custody of his own valuables; and that it might be vastly cheaper, as well as more effective, for the whole community of business men to combine, and assign the guardianship to one man, than for each to exercise it on his own account. Hence would result a building, centrally located, with strong vaults, and other safeguards and securities, where each person having surplus funds would deposit them for safe keeping.

It would not take long to learn that only a part of the money deposited would be likely to be withdrawn at one time. Hence a portion might be loaned temporarily. Experience and observation would furnish data for calculating how large this portion might be, and how much it would be necessary to keep constantly on hand. The part thus loaned on proper security, and made returnable at short intervals, would be paying interest; which would be a compensation for the care of the money, and also afford a profit. Such a disposition of the funds would also be an advantage to the community, by keeping its capital more fully employed. An arrangement of this kind would have all the elements of *a bank of deposit.*

3. We see that *credit* appears as an important factor in

this department of banking. It has a wider scope even here than has been indicated. The primary and natural process would be such, that, whenever a man had money to deposit, he would carry it to the bank, and the sum would be placed to his credit. Whenever he desired to use a portion of it, he would draw such a portion, and be debited with so much. But an abridgment of this process would come early into use. The depositor, having a debt to pay, instead of going to the bank, and drawing the money, and then paying it over to his creditor, would give the latter an order on the bank. The receiver might do one of three things with the order. He might draw the money; or he might deposit the order as so much cash, in which latter case there would be a transfer of credit from the account of the drawer of the order to that of its receiver; or, without going to the bank at all, he might hand the order over, as so much cash, to some one with whom he has dealing; and it might pass through several hands, paying as many debts, before finding its way to the bank, and even then being entered, up to the last holder's credit, without the use of any money. Usually, however, the order is carried to the bank by the party first receiving it, and is either paid in cash or placed to his credit. Such is the process of *transfer of credits by checks.* Much the larger proportion of the business of the banks and their customers in some communities is done in this way. Many wholesale firms in the cities receive most of their payments for goods in drafts; they make their payments in the same way: so that comparatively little cash is used by them, though their transactions amount to thousands of dollars a week. Credit is thus made to greatly supplement money as an instrument of exchange. There is a still further development of this substituted agency, in the method of loan and deposit, which will be set forth hereafter.

4. So far we have been considering the method of payment by transfer of credit, when there is only one bank in the community. But there may be more than one, and different individuals may be doing business with different banks. Let us see how payments may be made without money in such cases. Suppose, in a large village, A makes his deposits in one bank, and B in another. A receives in payment of a debt, or in exchange for goods, a check on the second bank. Instead of drawing the money from that bank, he puts it, with other drafts and with cash, in the first bank, where he makes his deposits ; and the whole is credited to him as so much money. B may also receive a check on the first bank, in the way of exchange : this check he will deposit in the second bank, where he does business. What these men do, a score or a hundred others may do. Thus there may be in each of these banks, or in each of half a dozen if there be so many, a number of checks upon each or all of the others. At the end of the day or of the week, each bank settles with every other, exchanging checks, and paying balances in money, or passing them over to a new account. Usually this balance is comparatively small, so that here again is an abridgment of the use of money by credit on a large scale.

5. In large cities, there are institutions called clearing-houses, for facilitating the settlement of checks and drafts between banks. They are of recent origin, but have already grown to be among the most important of financial agencies. Only a brief description of them can be given.

The clearing-house is a room where the several banks of a city send their representatives with the checks and drafts which each has on any of the others. We have already seen how one bank comes into possession of checks drawn on another. There are certain officers and employees of the clearing-house, who keep a record of the accounts between the several banks; and the work is thoroughly systematized. Each bank, before sending in its checks, assorts them in several parcels corresponding to the banks upon which they are drawn. On arriving at the clearing-house, the clerk presents them respectively to the several clerks of the clearing-banks. These checks have already been entered on the " out-clearing book;" that is, debited to the several banks on which they are drawn. Each bank-representative, on receiving the checks against his own bank, has them entered in the " in-clearing book." Opportunity is given for each bank to reject any checks which it does not see fit to pay; and, after all rectifications are made, each clerk reckons up the claims against his bank, and compares the amount with that in the out-clearing book, which indicates what is due from the other banks to it. The difference is the balance which this particular bank is to pay or receive, as the case may be. These balances are reported to the officers of the clearing-house, and invested in a kind of balance-sheet. The two sides should exactly balance, since whatever is received by one bank must have been paid by another. Of late, in London it has been the custom to pay the balances, not in cash, but in checks on the Bank of England, where each City bank ordinarily has an account. Thus transactions to the amount of $100,000,000 a day are settled without the intervention of any money at all. In the New-York clearing-house there have been exchanges effected in a single year to the amount of nearly $34,000,000,000, with cash balances of less than $1,500,000,000, or less than four per cent. That is, four dollars are made to do the work, which, without these agencies, it would require one hundred to accomplish.[1]

---

[1] See American Cyclopædia, article " Bank ; " also, Jevons's Money and the Mechanism of Exchange.

6. It is both curious and interesting to trace the process of exchange between remote parts of the same country or between different countries, and observe how large a proportion of it is effected by transfers of credit. Thus a man in Milwaukee consigns a thousand bushels of wheat to a firm in New York. He draws on that firm for one thousand dollars at ten days' sight. This is done, say, through the First National Bank of Milwaukee, which sends the draft to its correspondent bank in New York, say the Columbian Bank. The consignee pays the draft by a check on the Union Bank. The check finds its way to the clearing-house, where it is met by counter-checks, as we have seen; but the amount is credited by the Columbian Bank to the First National in Milwaukee, which in turn credits the same, less exchange, to the consignor of the wheat.

In the mean time another man in Milwaukee has ordered five hundred dollars' worth of carpeting from New York; and another, three hundred dollars' worth of boots and shoes; and still another, two hundred dollars' worth of cotton cloth. If these three persons all do business at the First National Bank of Milwaukee, they will, when their bills become due, deposit the amount of the same in this bank, which will give them drafts on the Columbian Bank of New York, and these will be sent to the parties in New York, to whom the bills are due; and the latter will deposit them in the banks where they do business. The drafts will come in due time through the clearing-house to the Columbian Bank, which will debit the several amounts to the First National in Milwaukee. Now there will be in the same bank a credit of a thousand dollars on account of the wheat received from Milwaukee, and a debit of a thousand dollars for the goods sent from New York. One amount offsets the other; and the wheat pays for the carpeting, cotton cloth, and boots and shoes.

It is very likely that the different buyers and sellers in Milwaukee may do business in different banks, each of which has a different correspondent bank in New York. The process in this case is more complicated: but even so, a very large proportion of these drafts and bills are met by other paper of the same kind, in some of the money-agencies East or West; so that, for the most part, the Western product pays for the Eastern merchandise. Of course more or less money passes back and forth, when the bills of exchange fail to meet; but the actual amount of cash used is very small in comparison with that of the business done. The same general features of the system of exchange by means of credit exist in international trade.

7. There are four kinds of banks, which it was my purpose to describe; namely, banks of deposit, savings-banks, banks of discount, and banks of issue or circulation. Sometimes these are all combined in one; and generally, in this country, the functions of three of them are performed by one institution. I have already described banks of deposit. Before going on to consider the banks of discount and circulation, which are closely connected with the former, let us see what is meant by a savings bank.

A *savings bank* is an institution in which small sums of money are deposited from time to time, as they accumulate in the hands of persons of small incomes and moderate earnings. The depositors are credited with these sums, and receive a certificate, usually in the form of a deposit-book. They are allowed a moderate amount of interest in any case, and an additional amount contingently. The bank loans out the money thus deposited, to trustworthy persons, in large sums, the rate of interest being somewhat higher than that regularly paid to the depositors. The benefit of such an institution is twofold. In the first place, there are many persons who have moderate sums of money, or property convertible into money, which they desire should be earning something in some safe place. The amount, by itself, is too small to be loaned to advantage. Such persons are not likely to know how, even if the sums at their disposal were sufficient, to find the best investment, or to determine concerning the security offered. But put in the hands of men who make this their business under rules devised by the best financial talent of the community, and who can combine these small sums, and invest them to the best advantage, it is made both safe and profitable for small capitalists.

In the second place, there are many who wish to unite their labor and skill with capital in some productive enterprise, and, having no capital of their own, desire to borrow. They do not always know the persons who have money to loan. The savings bank gives them an advantage which they would not otherwise have. It is thus a double benefit: first, to those who have some surplus, but would be unable to loan it to advantage; and, secondly, to those who are in want of capital, but would not know where to find it.

8. *Banks of discount and loan* are frequently combined with banks of deposit, though not necessarily so. They are usually constituted as follows: A charter from the Government is secured, reciting the privileges of the institution, and specifying the conditions to which it must be subject, its responsibilities, and the amount of capital required. This capital is divided into a certain number of shares. When the charter is secured, the books are opened for subscribers to the stock, of which some take more and some fewer shares. Each shareholder has a voice in the choice of directors, in proportion to the number of shares held by him. When the bank is organized, each stockholder pays in the amount subscribed by him. Under a specie-basis system, this is paid in silver and gold.

The principal functions of such a bank are exchange, discount, and loaning; all, as will be seen, being devices for systematizing and utilizing the credit of the community. Of the character of *exchange*, we already have some notion. Certain banks in different countries, or in remote parts of the same country, are in correspondence, and have accounts with one another. If a person in the vicinity of one of these banks wishes to pay a bill due in some distant place, he goes to the bank near him, and purchases a draft on some bank in a large central city, with which the local bank is in correspondence. This draft is sent to the creditor, who will doubtless deposit it in the bank with which he does business, where it will be paid, or its amount credited to him. It will sooner or later find its way, through other banks and the clearing-house, to the bank upon which it is drawn. This is the simple form and operation of a bill of exchange, but the process is often much more complicated. By reason of the correspondence of the country banks with those of the great commercial capitals, and of the latter with one another, a man in Mississippi may pay a debt in Ohio by a draft on New York; and a debt in Brussels or Geneva may be paid by a bill of exchange on London or Paris.

A partial notion of *discount* and *loaning* may be gathered from the following illustrations. When a wholesale merchant sells a quantity of goods to a customer, he may make out a bill payable in thirty, sixty, or ninety days, which the customer accepts, and thus binds himself to pay at the time stipulated. This bill, indorsed by himself, the wholesale merchant deposits in the bank with which he does business, and is credited with the amount of the bill, less interest for the time it is to run. A bill thus disposed of is said to be *discounted*. Sometimes a note is given by one person, and indorsed by another, and offered at the bank. If accepted, the amount is either paid over in money, or placed to the credit of the borrower. The interest is either paid when the note becomes due, or is deducted from the amount loaned in advance, usually the latter; and thus the term *discount* is used with reference to both kinds of transactions.

9. Before indicating further the operation of a bank of discount, it is desirable, since the two are ordinarily united, to describe a *bank of issue or circulation.* We have seen that the stock or capital of a bank, as banking is usually conducted on a specie basis, is supposed to consist of metallic coin. But as this would be inconvenient to carry about in large amounts, and as it is subject to much risk, the bank, instead of loaning its coin, loans its own notes, payable in specie on demand. As only a few persons would prefer specie to paper, as long as the latter will command the specie, the banks usually keep on hand only a certain proportion of the capital for the redemption of the notes, even though the notes in circulation call for an amount equal to the whole stock of the bank. The remainder may be so invested or loaned as to be earning a profit for its owners. That this usage has been sometimes grossly abused, is true; and in some parts of our country it has made banking a fraud, and a farce of the most disastrous character. A bank constituted as above indicated, and combining the three functions named, may loan and draw interest on its loans in three ways: (*a*) it may loan the larger part of its capital; (*b*) it may loan a considerable proportion of its deposits; (*c*) it may loan its own promises to pay, to the extent of half or two-thirds of its capital.

10. It is evident that banks deal not merely in money, but also in debts and credits, and in these latter to a much greater extent than in the former. A little further examination will make this clear. Sir John Lubbock, a noted English financier, gives an analysis of a sum of £19,000,000, paid into his banking-house in the city of London. It was composed of —

Checks and bills	£18,395,000
Bank-notes	487,000
Coin	118,000
	£19,000,000 [1]

Here it will be seen that only a little more than three per cent of the transactions of the bank involved the use of any kind of money, and only one-fifth of that money was coin. In an ordinary country bank, or even in a bank of almost any city of moderate size, the proportion of money used will be considerably greater than this; but, in any case, it will constitute only a small part of the business.

It is not to be inferred that banks can be made to substitute the instrumentality of money altogether. They constitute an agency through which wholesale dealers, capitalists, employers, and men engaged in extensive enterprises, can manage their exchanges with comparatively little money. But men in moderate circumstances — small farmers, mechanics, and inhabitants of sparsely settled regions — must make a much larger proportion of their exchanges by means of money. Hence a real scarcity of money may be a far greater misfortune to the latter classes than to the former.

[1] Jevons's Money and Mechanism of Exchange.

CHAPTER XI.

THE PAPER CURRENCY OF THE UNITED STATES.

1. THE system of banking created by our General Government during the time of the civil war differs somewhat from that which previously existed, and which has been already described. In the first place, under the former system the banks were chartered by the legislatures of their respective States. This may still be the case; but the General Government now imposes on the circulation of the State banks a heavy tax from which that of the National banks is exempt. The result has been what it was intended to be; namely, to discourage all circulation except that of the National banks or those chartered by the General Government.

In the second place, all the notes of the National banks are guaranteed, as to their ultimate redemption, by the Government, and yet not at its risk. Every banking association must, at its organization, deliver to the United-States treasurer interest-bearing bonds of the Nation, equal in value to two-thirds of the capital. It is then furnished by the comptroller of the currency with circulating notes of various denominations, in blank, equal in amount to ninety per cent of the current market-value of the bonds deposited, but not exceeding the par value of such bonds. In any case of the failure of the bank, there is no risk of loss to the holders of its notes, as they are good for the face of them at the United-

States Treasury. The Treasury also incurs no risk, as it has in its possession securities of the bank to something more than the extent of the whole circulation, in the form of United-States bonds. The bank loses nothing by depositing these securities, since the Government is paying the interest on them.

It is this feature, with one other soon to be mentioned, which gives the notes of these banks the character of a truly national currency. The bills of a bank in Minnesota or Texas are just as acceptable in New York or in Maine as the bills of the banks of the latter States. Under the old system, a bank-note in most of the States could hardly circulate out of the vicinity of the place of its issue. This was the source of endless annoyance to a traveller, and frequently of expense by way of exchange.

In the third place, these National-bank notes are a legal tender in the payment of all dues to the United States, except import duties; and also for all dues from the United States, except interest on the public debt. But they are not a legal tender for private dues.

Again, the National banks are required to keep on hand, for the redemption of their notes, a certain proportion of "lawful money." This proportion differs in different places. Sixteen of the principal cities are designated, in which it is fixed at twenty-five per cent. Elsewhere it is fifteen per cent.

I have given the main features of the National-bank system as distinguished from that of State banks which existed previous to the civil war. That the former is a very great improvement on the latter, there can be no question. That it has its imperfections, is undoubtedly true.

2. Besides the National-bank notes, Government notes have, for something over twenty years, formed a large part of

the instrument of exchange. The "greenback," popularly so called from the color of the ink with which the back is printed, is a promissory note of the United-States Government, drawing no interest, and made by law a legal tender for all dues except duties on imports and interest on the public debt. These notes began to be issued early in the time of the civil war. The national treasury was empty, the banks had suspended specie payment, industry everywhere was paralyzed; immense sums of money were needed to supply the implements and munitions of war, and the sustenance, clothing, and equipment of the soldiers; and it was impossible instantly to effect a loan, such as would enable the Government to meet the demands upon it. It was a desperate emergency, and required bold and decisive, if not desperate, action. It was not without precedent for a Government to issue its own promises to pay, though with the understanding that the fulfilment of the promise must be indefinitely postponed, and to make these a legal tender constituting them a part of the "lawful money" of the nation. They became, and still remain, a part of the debt incurred by the war.

The immediate effect of the measure was most beneficial. It not only furnished funds for carrying on the war, and was thus perhaps the salvation of the nation; but it provided a circulating medium and instrument of exchange, which set in motion at once the commerce and industry which had been languishing, and produced wholesome activity where previously there had been general stagnation. In connection with other financial measures adopted about the same time, it became the occasion of remarkably prosperous conditions, in spite of the derangements incident to the war. It has been said that these conditions were largely fictitious, and that the revulsion and protracted depression of the next decade were both the proof of this and the natural consequence of such a measure. But the fact that almost the whole commercial world, except France, suffered equally severe depression at the same time, would seem to militate against this hypothesis. It is remarkable, too, that France had a currency, and was under financial conditions, similar to our own.

3. The advantages of a paper currency are numerous and important, but they may be grouped as follows : —

1. Paper is more convenient than specie for handling and carrying. A hundred dollars in silver, or a thousand in gold, could be carried about the person with neither ease nor safety.

2. The wear and tear of specie would be much more costly by constant use than that of paper.

3. It forms· a supplementary currency which is of vast advantage to a community. Were all the exchanges to be made through the medium of coin, without the intervention of credit in the form of paper, commerce would be greatly impeded. There is not enough gold and silver in the commercial world to answer this purpose. The financial history of the modern world shows this. Hence the necessity of credit, which, in civilized nations, performs far more of the functions of an instrument of exchange than gold and silver. A considerable part of this credit element consists of what we have called paper money.

It is generally acknowledged that the first two advantages mentioned above constitute valid reasons for the use of paper money. But the third is rejected by a certain class, on the ground that bank-notes should never be used to supplement coin. This class holds that only so much paper money should be issued from the banks, or any other source, as is equivalent in the amount promised to the amount of coin actually on hand by the issuer; so that, if all the notes were presented at one time, they could be redeemed at once. This would, of course, make the bank-notes of no advantage whatever as a supplementary currency. It is claimed, on the other hand, that these notes are entirely safe under careful regulations, where not less than one-third as much coin is kept on hand as the notes called for.

The evils of paper money are found chiefly in the liability to an expansion and contraction of the currency, the power of which is largely in the hands of the managers of the banks, or, in the case of governmental notes, under the direction of the national legislature. Such fluctuations are productive of serious disasters to commerce, and to all the interests of industry.

Book Fourth

DISTRIBUTION.

CHAPTER I.

GENERAL STATEMENT.

1. By distribution is meant *the determination of the proportion of the value of any product to which each contributor to that product is entitled.* In such a determination many considerations are involved. There are the various kinds of labor, such as physical and mental, common and skilled, the more and the less efficient; together with such modifications of these as are implied in their being mingled in different proportions, and in the experience, aptitude, and culture of individuals.

Let us take some one product, — say this table, — and consider the number of laborers and the variety of labor contributing to its production. Those who transformed the lumber and other materials are only a very small proportion of these contributors. There are also those who manufactured the lumber, those who cut the logs out of which it was made, and those who hauled them to the mill; the makers of the nails, and of the iron from which the nails were made; the miners who got out the ore, and the transporters of the same; the painter, the producers of the paint and the oil, and all that lies back of this; and, in addition, the maker of all the tools and machinery used in all these operations; and much else that we cannot specify. Evidently the three or four dollars, at which the completed table is valued, must be distributed among, perhaps, two or three scores of persons who have had a hand, directly or indirectly, in its production. The question is, How shall we equitably apportion this amount among these several parties?

2. The most natural answer to this question would undoubtedly be, that each individual engaged in the production of a valuable commodity is entitled to an exact equivalent of the value by him produced. If it were simply estimating the respective shares of several laborers of about equal ability, it would be a very easy matter. If it related to several laborers differing only in physical strength and skill, it might be clearly within the ordinary powers of computation. The problem might be calculable, even if we had to take into account certain differences of intellectual competency; but when we remember that not only are all these elements, and many more pertaining to personal labor, to enter into the question in countless complications, but that capital, in a vast variety of forms, comes into co-operation with all productive effort everywhere, then the situation is seen to be environed with many and great difficulties.

3. The following is the general division of the subject : —

1. Wages, or the compensation of labor.

2. Profits, or the compensation of employers and proprietors.

3. Interest, or the compensation for the use of capital, reckoned as money.

4. Rent, or the compensation for land.

5. Taxes, or the compensation for the services of the government.

The term "compensation" is not used with scientific precision, and may mislead. It is simply intended to signify the shares to which the several co-operating parties are entitled by reason of their relations to the product. It is not necessary to suppose that these different kinds of compensation are always distributed to as many different parties. For instance, a farmer, especially in this country, may own his farm free from debt. What might otherwise be interest and rent, now becomes scarcely distinguishable from profit. He may also be his own hired man, and so receive the wages which he would otherwise pay to another. He manages and owns his stock and entire capital; and thus all the product, except the share due the government, is properly taken by himself.

CHAPTER II.

WAGES: GENERAL VIEW.

1. THOUGH wages have been represented as the compensation for labor, the term has, in ordinary usage, a somewhat more limited signification. It indicates that which is paid to those who labor under an employer, and have no other interest in the business except to secure steady work and satisfactory remuneration. It has also a still narrower meaning, as being the reward of services performed by the day or month, as distinguished from salaried employees, such as clerks, superintendents, teachers, and clergymen; also, as distinguished from those whose service is paid in the form of fees, as lawyers, physicians; and from those who are compensated by commissions.

2. The theory of labor and wages, held by many writers in Great Britain, and by some in this country, is that of a *laboring-class*, who furnish the labor, and who are paid out of what is called a *wages-fund*. The capital of the community is regarded as a real, but rather indefinite and gradually increasing, quantity of wealth. It is supposed to exist in the four forms of land, material, implements and machinery, and the wages-fund. This last is reckoned as fixed for the time, and devoted to the payment of labor. The problem of the rate of wages thus involves two factors; namely, the number of laborers, and the amount of the

wages-fund. The former is the divisor, and the latter the dividend; the quotient is the rate of wages at any time possible. If the number of laborers increase, the fund remaining the same, wages must diminish. If the fund increases or diminishes, the number of laborers remaining the same, wages increase or diminish correspondingly. Thus, we are told, every thing is determined by natural, inflexible laws; and no matter how low the wages may be, or how hard the lot of the laboring-man, there is no remedy.

Now, the existence of natural economical laws is not to be doubted. But it should be borne in mind, that these laws, even when correctly ascertained, may be almost infinitely varied in their operation by various forms of human influence. Whether, in this case, the law has been correctly ascertained, we shall see hereafter.

3. It is this habit of regarding laborers as a class, that affects the philosophy of some of even the most philanthropic writers on this subject. There is nothing in the nature of the case that necessitates this. In the Northern States of this country, among the native American population, there is, properly speaking, no laboring-class. A large proportion of the citizens begin life on their own account, by working for wages. Many of these become capitalists in a small way, by saving their earnings, and, after a little, begin to carry on business for themselves. To a great extent they are clearly independent, even while acting as laborers; and it is not uncommon to find a hired man with both more means and more ability and intelligence than his employer. Into the mind of such a laborer, there never comes the thought that he occupies an inferior social position. He is simply in the relation of one who has service to sell, and he stands in the market on the same footing as the farmer, or the manufacturer, or the merchant, who offer their wares, and

invite the public to purchase. It is true that this condition is not universal here. There is an occasional tendency to the degradation of labor through the ignorance or poverty of the laborer, and by the opportunities furnished to the employer to take advantage, such as the average selfishness of humanity would prompt him to use.

4. But even on the theory of a laboring-class, there must be a minimum rate of wages; that is, a rate below which capital itself would suffer detriment. Even among ordinary laborers, the lowest wages which can be permanently maintained must be at least sufficient to support a married pair in good working-order, and enable them to bring up not less than two children. If the wages are not enough for this, then the capitalist must sooner or later suffer damage. For, if the laborer have so little food or clothing or shelter that his physical health is impaired, his labor will be less productive. Unless there be so many children coming to maturity as to keep up the full number of laborers, there must be a decrease of production, to the detriment of the capitalist as well as of the whole community. There is, moreover, to be taken into account the liability to sickness and accident; also the fact of old age, when the ability to labor diminishes or ceases. Wages which are adjusted to these conditions are the lowest possible in any kind of reason. Whether *such* wages would be, economically, the most desirable, even for the employer and the capitalist, will be considered hereafter. There are reputable economists whose theories oblige them to regard this as the point to which wages naturally tend, and who hold that above, or much above, this they cannot permanently rise. The argument is, that higher wages, even if compatible with the interests of capital, would cause too great an increase of population; thus making the ratio of the latter to capital smaller, and so causing again a diminution of wages.

CHAPTER III.

WAGES AS AFFECTED BY VARIOUS CIRCUMSTANCES.

1. We are to distinguish between *nominal wages* and *real wages*. The former indicates the amount of *money* received for a certain amount of labor; the latter has reference to the quantity of *commodities* which the money received for the labor will purchase. If a man had received a dollar a day in 1860, but received in 1870 a dollar and a half for the same work, it does not necessarily follow that wages were fifty per cent. higher in the latter than in the former case. This might or might not be true; but it certainly would not, if the purchasing power of money were nearly twice as great in 1860 as in 1870.

2. There are various conditions to be taken into account in estimating the real value of wages, even when the nominal amount is clearly understood. Sometimes laborers contract to take their pay in commodities furnished by the employer, or on his order; and it is frequently the fact, that the real value of these is less than if the purchaser had ready money in hand, and a choice of markets.

There are also cases where work can be had only a part of the year, as those of stone-masons and roof-tinners. If the daily wages are twice as high as in ordinary trades, while work can be had only half as many days in the year, the real earnings are only the same.

3. There are some conditions affecting wages, which are different from those just mentioned. There is, first, the agreeableness of the employment. This has no small influence in determining wages: men will work for less in an occupation where the work is to their taste and the associaations are pleasant, than where it is against their inclinations, or in any way repugnant to them. Some occupations imply higher compensation, from the fact of the greater difficulty of preparation for them. I do not now refer to merely those which require a marked, or more than ordinary, natural ability, or superior education; though it is true of them also. But there are certain trades to which years of toil must be devoted, and sometimes much expense incurred, in order to their acquirement.

One other circumstance which affects wages is the amount of trust and confidence which the employed receive from the employer. A confidential clerk in a great business house receives a large salary. The wages paid to an engineer in an extensive factory, or to any other workman upon whom the lives of many persons, the safety and efficiency of the machinery, and the regular on-going of a vast establishment depend, are likely to be much greater than those paid to persons upon whom no such responsibility rests, even though the labor of the latter may be far more toilsome than that of the former.

4. The influence of the industrial system of a community on wages is very great. A section in which agriculture is almost the exclusive occupation will be characterized, other things being equal, by low wages. The same will be true of a community where there is a small variety of industries. In the northern counties of England, particularly in Yorkshire and Northumberland, the wages of the agricultural laborer in the late autumn and the early winter are thirteen or fourteen shillings a week; while for the same kind of labor in the south-western counties of Dorsetshire and Wiltshire, the wages average less than nine shillings. The difference is not in the nominal, as distinguished from the real, wages. The reason for this variation of more than forty per cent is found in the fact, that one of these districts has a great diversity of employments, while the other is almost exclusively agricultural.

CHAPTER IV.

HIGH AND LOW WAGES AS RELATED TO DEAR AND CHEAP LABOR.

1. As we have seen, it is not the amount of money received for labor that determines whether wages are high or low; so, on the other hand, labor is counted dear or cheap, not by the amount of money paid for it, but by the amount of valuable product secured for the money paid. An employer may buy a day's work of one man for a dollar and a half, and of another for a dollar, just as he may buy one axe for two dollars, and another for one dollar. But in both cases the higher-priced may be the cheaper. The two-dollar axe may be of three times the service that the one-dollar one is, and the dollar-and-a-half laborer may effect twice as much as the one who works for a dollar.

There is another way, not always taken, of looking at this subject. Low wages are sometimes the cause of inefficient labor, as well as the latter of the former. Looking at the matter in this light, it is possible that capitalists and employers may find some way to avoid the difficulty of the wages question without more sacrifice than will result in their ultimate advantage.

2. The theory of a *necessary rate* of wages, if rigidly adhered to, would utterly preclude all hope of any substantial improvement in the condition of laborers. They are, according to this theory, doomed to remain at the point where the rewards of labor are just sufficient to keep them in fair working-order on the one hand, and meagre enough on the other to prevent their increasing faster than the increase of capital. But is there not a possibility that this " necessary rate " might keep the laborer at some point below that of the highest efficiency practicable to him as even a mere human machine?

" Looking upon a human laborer, then, as we would upon a steam-engine, we see that the amount of force which he is capable of creating depends upon the amount of food supplied to him; a part of it answering the purpose of the coal which gives heat, another answering to the water which is converted into steam and generates motion. A sheet-iron jacket put around the boiler prevents the waste of heat in one case, just as a woollen jacket about the body of the laborer does in the other. But food, clothing, and shelter are supplied to the human machine in the shape of wages. To stint them, and to keep the laborer down to the lowest point that will induce him to live, without deterring him from propagation, is precisely the same kind of economy which would keep the steam-engines of a nation at half their working-power to save wood and water and sheet-iron. The rate of wages which such considerations would demand has been attained in very few regions of the world. Suppose it anywhere to have been reached: the laborer is only brought up to the condition of an ox. But he has intelligence, which the ox has not; and it is the great element of his industrial power. In the lowest description of labor, there is occasion for judgment in the selection of means, in the modes of exerting force most advantageously, and in the adoption of tools and simple mechanical principles to economize time and strength." [1]

[1] E. P. Smith's Political Economy, p. 107.

Clearly enough, economy does not require us to secure any kind of labor or laborers that can be had at the lowest price, but to secure that labor which will produce the most at the least expense. If a man whose nerves and muscles are in the best condition because his means of subsistence are ample, whose hope of securing a competence gives him vigor, enterprise, and self-respect, and whose intelligence and prudence enable him to see a hundred ways of economizing productive conditions and avoiding waste, demands large wages, — who does not see that it is better for his employer to meet this demand, than to give half or a quarter as much for an ignorant, hopeless, under-fed human animal?

CHAPTER V.

"THE WAGES-FUND."

1. THE doctrine of the wages-fund has been stated in Chapter II., **2.** The only remedy for low wages, according to it, is such restraints as will keep the ratio of population to capital below a given point. Any increase of the former beyond that diminishes wages. If it increase much, the wages will be so low that subsistence will be insufficient, and population will be checked. There is no other alternative. The laborers must carefully limit the size of their families, or suffer the direful consequences of want and famine. It would not be so bad if each one had only to govern himself, in order to reap the fruit of his own prudence. But it is of no account for one or a few to do this, unless there is a general co-operation of laborers. Consequently such a remedy is impracticable; consequently, too, there is no remedy: there is the natural rate of wages, and there is no legitimate possibility of any general or permanent change for the better. For if capital increase, no matter how rapidly, the increase of wages could be only temporary; since, according to the theory, this increase would occasion an increase of population, speedily restoring the old ratio.

2. We have already seen that the amount of product, and consequently of profit, is not necessarily inversely as wages. The very smallness of the wages sometimes makes the product not only smaller, but *proportionally* smaller. When wages are at the point where they barely keep the laborer in good working-condition, a diminution of them will simply subtract from his producing-power, with no advantage to the employer.

3. Another argument against the theory under consideration is set forth by Professor F. A. Walker with great clearness. He denies the doctrine that wages are paid out of capital. The assumption thus contradicted lies at the basis of the theory, and is the vicious, though plausible, element in it. It is true that capital is often drawn upon for the advance of wages. But even this is not always the case. Every one who is acquainted with business knows that there are many enterprises in which the workmen draw only a small portion, and sometimes none, of their wages till there are returns from the sale of the product.

"It is the prospect of a profit in production which determines the employer to hire laborers; and it is the anticipated value of the product that determines how much he can pay them. The product, then, and not capital, furnishes at once the motive to employment, and the measure of wages. If this be so, the whole wage-fund theory falls; for it is built on the assumption that capital furnishes the measure of wages. The wage-fund is no larger because of the lack of capital, and the only way to increase the aggregate amount is to increase capital." [1]

4. Professor Walker shows further, that the theory takes no account of the quality of laborers, and is thereby seriously at fault. Suppose there is a certain amount of capital which is set apart for wages. Now, according to the dogma, this is the dividend, and the number of laborers is the divisor which is to determine the quotient, that is, the rate of

[1] The Wages Question, p. 144.

wages. It will make no difference, according to the theory, whether these laborers are the better class of English and American workmen, or the worse class of Irish or East Indians whose efficiency averages less than one-fourth that of the former: the wages must be the same!

CHAPTER VI.

CAREY'S LAW OF THE INCREASE OF WAGES.

1. Mr. Carey has developed what he regards as a grand law governing the relations of labor to capital in every well-ordered society. This principle is also supported by Bastiat, one of the leading French economists, and by others of note. It may be stated as follows: As society advances, the laborer's *proportion* of the joint product of labor and capital tends steadily to increase; the *proportion* of the capitalist tends steadily to decline; while the *quantity* assigned to both steadily increases. This is in accordance with the principle already illustrated, that, as society improves (at least up to a certain point, which no nation has yet reached), both wealth and population increase, but the former faster than the latter.

2. Let us look at some apparent manifestations of this principle. The savage who has invented a bow and arrow, with which he can secure as much game in a day as before in a week, may loan them to a neighbor on the condition of receiving for their use three-quarters of the product. This may seem like an enormous profit; but to the borrower, even at that rate, it is a very great advantage; since, after paying for the use of the implements, he still has twice as much game as he could have secured without them. But, as other men construct bows and arrows, there is a competition among the capitalists; and the instruments begin to be loaned at the price of two-thirds, one-half, one-quarter, and one-tenth or twentieth of the product. As other inventions come in, the same thing will occur in respect to them; namely, that capital will be having an always diminishing, and labor an always increasing, proportion of the joint product. The first fishing-net, the first canoe, and the first rude cutting-instrument bring large compensation for their use; but they will prepare the way for others which will not only be improvements on their predecessors, but, by reason of their multiplication, will command less and less compensation.

3. Take as an illustration the cutting instrument. Poor as was the axe of stone, its utility was very great. The canoe, which could not be constructed at all without it, gave great increase of power to the owner. Another than the owner of the axe can well afford to pay the latter three-quarters of all he can produce by the use of it, for the one-fourth falling to his own share is much more than he could secure without it.

After a time the bronze axe is invented, and proves far more useful. The stone axe is still in use; but its value has greatly depreciated, since the same amount — or probably a smaller amount — of labor is requisite to the production of the bronze axe. For this reason the owner of the latter will loan it for something less than the proportion previously received for the stone axe, say for two-thirds the product. As this product will be at least twice as great as before, both the laborer and the capitalist are benefited; the former receiving a larger proportion as well as a large amount of the product, while the latter receives also a larger amount, though a smaller proportion. The comparative effects of the later and earlier distribution are as follows: —

Stage.	Total Product.	Laborer's Share.	Capitalist's Share.
First	4	1	3
Second	8	$2\frac{2}{3}$	$5\frac{1}{3}$

"The reward of labor has more than doubled, being an increased proportion of an increased quantity. The capitalist's share has not quite doubled, he receiving a diminished proportion of an increased quantity. The portion of the laborer, which had been at first as one to three, is now as one to two, with great increase of power to become himself a capitalist."

The axe of iron now being invented, and being the product of less labor than the axe of bronze, but having at the same time far greater utility, its owner will be content with a still smaller *proportion*, while he will receive a still larger *amount* of the product. So of the axe of steel, coming after that of iron: its cost will be less, while its product will be more. The capitalist will find an augmentation of his share of the product, but his proportion will be still less than before. Both the proportion and the amount falling to the laborers will be enhanced. The following table will represent the whole process of the operation of the law: —

	Total Product.	Laborer's Share.	Capitalist's Share.
Axe of stone	4	1	3
Axe of bronze	8	$2\frac{2}{3}$	$5\frac{1}{3}$
Axe of iron	16	8	8
Axe of steel	32	$19\frac{2}{10}$	$12\frac{8}{10}$

Of course, this is but an imperfect representation of the operation of this principle, but it is exemplified in a great variety of facts in the relations of human society. It is not a mere theory, beautiful and wholesome in idea but practically inoperative. The whole history of labor in its relation to capital, whether in the form of wages or rent or interest, indicates more or less clearly its existence. It is not intended to assert that it operates palpably everywhere and under all sorts of conditions. The bad policies adopted by communities, or the surrender of general to class interests, may counteract this as well as any other natural tendency. But, in an advancing civilization and a prosperous community, this law is nearly certain to manifest itself.

4. No one can reasonably doubt that real wages have been advancing in all the civilized nations during the last three or four centuries. That the laboring-men in most of the European countries are, as a general rule, better fed, clad, and housed now than they were a century ago, and that they were then better off than in the previous century, can easily be made evident. Says McCulloch, himself a disciple of Ricardo and Malthus, "Let any one compare the state of this or any European country with what it was five hundred, or even one hundred, years ago, and he will be satisfied that prodigious advances have been made; that the means of subsistence have increased much more rapidly than the population; and that the laboring-population are now generally in possession of conveniences and luxuries that were formerly not enjoyed by the richest lords." This is more conspicuously true in France than in England.

CHAPTER VII.

REMEDIES FOR LOW WAGES.

1. ARE there any real remedies for the evils which are still incident to our system of labor? If the theory of wages which we have been examining is correct, there would seem to be no help. Yet, since great improvements *have been* going on for some centuries, and as these have taken place without violating any natural law, and even in opposition to many adverse theories, and in spite of social, governmental, and other unnatural obstacles, it is pretty nearly certain that there must be some economic principles in accordance with which general and constant improvement may come.

2. The extent to which the government may interfere to promote the interests of the laborer is a question of some importance. If the doctrine held by the extreme school of British economists is correct, — namely, that government has no functions except those implied in maintaining justice, — that settles the question. But there are very few of even this school who accept the extreme consequences of their premises. It is generally admitted, that it is the duty of the government to see that every man has a fair chance to dispose of his labor to the best advantage. No one should be arbitrarily excluded from privileges which under the same circumstances others are permitted to enjoy. Fair and equal competition is not to be complained of; but unequal competition, caused or occasioned by obstacles which government can remove, should not be permitted. Government cannot fix the rate of wages, or the prices of commodities, or do any thing necessarily implying either of these; but there are some things that come naturally within its province.

It may provide for general education; it may also, to a considerable extent, furnish opportunity for technical education. It can prevent the employment of young children in factories and shops; both that they may have opportunity for education, and for other economical reasons. It may make sanitary regulations in the interests of laborers, both in respect to the rooms and buildings in which labor is to be performed, and in respect to tenements and lodging-houses. It may, too, within certain limits, regulate the hours of labor; though these limits would probably differ under different circumstances. There is, of course, a possibility of uneconomical as well as economical action here.

3. A supposed remedy for low wages, to which resort is often had, is that of a " strike." This is simply a combination of workmen to make a demand upon their employers concerning wages and other conditions, and a refusal to work unless their demands are met. If the workmen are united, and remain firm, unless the employer can secure other workmen, the latter must accede to the conditions, or his whole capital must lie idle at no small loss, until one party yield, or some compromise is effected.

Strikes have been summarily condemned by many persons. Of course, if the theory of a rigid natural rate of wages is correct, strikes are not only useless, but every way harmful. Whether, in the case of the incorrectness of that theory, such combinations are effective of any good, is an open question. That laborers as well as employers may find some advantage in combination, is not doubtful. The very fact that there is a liability of such combinations, is of itself an inducement to employers to avoid all occasions for them.

On the other hand, there are on the side of the laborers many obstacles to success by this device. It is not always practicable to make the combination so general but that other laborers can be secured in the place of those in the strike. Again, there is a great loss of time, and therefore of wages. Those who earn only enough to support themselves from day to day have no store laid by, and therefore must depend on the earnings of the more fortunate. It is of the essence of a successful strike, that all who engage in it be able to hold out. To this end, those who have saved any thing must share with those who have nothing. It thus becomes a question of average means, and this is pitted against the usually still greater means of employers. The chances are against success, and yet success is not impossible. There are cases in which the employers are compelled to yield. But even in the event of success, the loss may be greater than the gain. Dr. John Watts [1] illustrates the losses and gains of a *successful strike*. "Assuming five per cent addition to existing wages to be the matter in dispute between the employers and the laborers, he shows, that, *if the strike succeeds*, its results will be, roughly speaking, as follows : —

The loss of 1 lunar month's wages will require, to make it up, 1⅜ years of work at the extra rate.

The loss of 2 lunar months' wages will require, to make it up, 3½ years of work at the extra rate.

The loss of 6 lunar months' wages will require, to make it up, 9⅔ years of work at the extra rate.

The loss of 12½ lunar months' wages will require, to make it up 20 years of work at the extra rate.

[1] See Professor F. A. Walker: The Wages Question, pp. 30, 31.

"The strike of the London builders in 1859 was for ten per cent of time, or its equivalent, ten per cent of wages, and, as it lasted twenty-six weeks, would, if successful, have required ten and two-fifths years of continuous work at the extra rate to make up the loss of wages sacrificed."

There are other losses implied in a strike. A period of idleness is likely to furnish occasion for the formation of bad habits which may be a permanent detriment to the laborer. The circumstances are also apt to engender bad blood, and this is economically as well as otherwise a damage. The loss of the employer is always something; and this is a diminution of the capital of the community, and, so far forth, harmful to the laborer. Further, the diminution of product occasions enhancement of value; and this, if general, is a virtual reduction of wages.

It thus appears that strikes are not an unmixed good, even when successful. When unsuccessful, they are a serious misfortune. On the other hand, they are not an unmixed evil. They do sometimes effect that at which they aim. The fact that they are possible, and even actual, is a perpetual advantage to the laborer in every contest to which he is liable with the employer.

4. *Trades-unions* are a more permanent form of combination than strikes. They embrace usually only laborers of the same trade. They have two general objects. In the first place, they serve the purposes of mutual aid. Information is diffused, the sick and disabled are assisted, and any case of unusual hardship or oppression becomes the interest of the whole. So far they are, or at least may be, of great advantage. As a means of mutual defence, encouragement, and intelligence, they add to the value of man, tend to the increase of production, and secure for the laborer a constantly growing proportion of the joint product of labor and capital.

In the second place, a trades-union contemplates such an organization of its members as will have a direct influence upon their wages. There is a purpose to compass directly, and sometimes by questionable means, such a rise of wages as can only come about in accordance with fixed economical principles. One of the methods used is, to restrict the number of laborers in a particular trade. Some unions have rules designed to effect this limitation. Only a certain number of apprentices are to be permitted. Employers must not admit new workmen except under certain specified conditions, and only so many within such and such times The motive is to keep the number of laborers so small that wages shall be as high as possible. It may be temporarily advantageous, possibly permanently so in a few cases; just as it is advantageous to a company of capitalists to obtain control of the whole supply of a commodity for which there is a large demand, and thus keep the trade in their own hands, and prevent free competition. In the one case, as in the other, the supply is smaller than if there were no restriction, and the price of the article is greater. In the case of the trades-union, by limiting the number of laborers, the product is diminished, and the price is increased, making a doubly bad economical result

5. *Co-operative association* has been largely urged of late as a remedy for the disadvantages of workingmen By co-operative association pure and simple, is meant the carrying-on of a business enterprise on such terms that profits shall be wholly divided among the laborers, in proportion to the contribution of each to the product. There have been some remarkable and successful experiments in this direction within the last thirty years; but the most of these, and especially the most conspicuous, have been not in productive, but in commercial, enterprises. One of these has had a

fame extending over the civilized world; namely, that of the Rochdale Association. This combination has unquestionably been a successful one, and greatly advantageous to its members and patrons. It has been thought, because of the success of this and some other but inferior instances of commercial co-operation, that the principle could be applied to manufacturing industry. There have been some experiments in this direction, and with a certain degree of success in England. Yet, as I have understood, the co-operation has not extended to all the laborers, only to those furnishing capital; so that, after all, they have been of the nature of joint-stock companies.

6 Among the difficulties in the way of productive co-operation are to be reckoned the reverses to which all business is liable, and which require a considerable reserve of capital in order that they may be safely tided over. Experienced business men have estimated, that, on the average, about one year in six there will be no profit in most kinds of manufacturing, and there may be a considerable loss. The profits of the other five years have to make up this deficiency. Now, if there is only capital enough to carry on the business in these prosperous years, there will be in the adverse years, not only no profits to be divided, but there may a failure of wages.

Another more serious difficulty is found in the nature and requirements of what has all along been spoken of as the *employer*.[1] The employer is to be distinguished from the *capitalist*, with whom he is often confounded. The functions of both may co-exist in the same individual, but they are not identical. The employer must be a man *competent to conduct business*. He must be an organizer, not merely a

[1] See F. A. Walker: The Wages Question; also Political Economy, by the same author.

superintendent or overseer; but he must have the skill and the ability to put labor and capital together so as to render them profitably productive. He must also have several other qualities that do not often come together in one person, — good financial ability, a quick discernment and ready judgment in buying and selling, an accurate perception of the wants of the public both in character and extent, and many other things. He may be without capital of his own; and yet, whether a capitalist or not, he is a "captain of industry," and just as essential to the carrying-forward of productive enterprises as the commander of an army to the conduct of a campaign.

There are only a few persons in whom all these conditions meet. But such men are as essential to the laborers as they are to the capitalist, and they cannot be furnished to order from either class. Here, then, is the difficulty. Where the industry is free, and all have something like a fair chance, the employer generally and naturally comes to his place. I do not assert that there are no mere wage-laborers who are not as competent to be employers, in the sense in which that term is here used, as many who now essay to exercise that function. But there is, in the co operative system, no natural method of ascertaining such a functionary. There must be experiment, and experiments in such a case are costly. A single unsuccessful one would be disastrous: two successive failures would most likely prove fatal.

7. *Co-partnership of industry* has sometimes been tried by employers and proprietors with gratifying results. Laborers may be admitted to a participation in the profits which are realized through their own industry. Professor Fawcett[1] discusses this device in an interesting way. I avail myself of some of his illustrations. The reluctance of em-

---

[1] Manual of Political Economy, pp. 250–253.

ployers to concede the demands of their workmen for the increase of wages, is based upon the supposition that every such increase diminishes by just so much their profits. This has been the settled opinion of some economists. It has been shown in previous sections, that this is by no means always the case. Other instances go to show its incorrectness.

One of the illustrations of the advantage of co-partnership in production is that of M. Leclaire, a house-decorator in Paris. He employed about two hundred workmen, and had become greatly discouraged with the apathy and carelessness which they manifested, subjecting him to constant loss and annoyance. He therefore proposed to give them some pecuniary interest in the work, hoping to inspire in them a higher ambition with reference to it. He called them together, and told them he would continue to pay them the customary wages, and at the end of the year would distribute among them a certain share of the profits realized. The plan worked admirably; and M. Leclaire declared not only that he was otherwise satisfied, but that he was in a pecuniary sense abundantly recompensed for the share of the profits given to the workmen. Nor is this unnatural. It accords with the principle previously set forth. Larger remuneration often adds to the efficiency of the laborer; and this implies larger product, and consequently more to be distributed. In the case before us, there is an additional reason for a larger product, and hence a larger profit. There is the motive to save material and tools, and to make the most possible out of what is furnished. Much is also saved in the matter of superintendence. The cost of overseeing laborers who are interested only to receive their wages, and are careless whether the employer realizes much or little from their work, is usually very great. But when the employee has a direct interest in the product, there is less liability to shirk or to waste, and a greater inducement to make every thing tell for the interest of the enterprise. In such a case, labor largely superintends itself, and the expense otherwise incurred is added to the profits.

8. *The wages of women.* A social phenomenon which few have failed to observe is that of the difference between the wages of women and those of men in similar employments. At first sight the fact seems out of harmony with the general laws of political economy, yet the apparent discord is not altogether inexplicable.

There are several reasons why the wages of women are lower than those of men. One, and perhaps the most influential of these, is that the supply of the kind of service which women offer in the market is much greater in proportion to the demand for it, than is the kind of labor offered by men. Let us look at this a little more particularly. Owing to what seems to many a vice of our social system, the *variety* of labor which women have to offer for wages is very limited, while the *amount* is very great. There are comparatively few occupations to which women are admitted. Hence the number of women who have labor to sell, though not so great as that of men, is yet far greater in proportion to the work they are permitted to do. The occupations open to them become densely crowded, and the competition among those seeking wages is very great. In the very nature of things, the wages are lower than they otherwise would be. Housework, millinery and dressmaking, general sewing, some service in shops, fancy work, and teaching have been till recently, for the most part, the occupations to which women have been admitted. Because women must work in these if at all, the supply of labor has become so great that the wages in them must be smaller than if the demand were to the supply the same as in the case of men.

Another obstacle to the improvement of women's wages lies in the fact that it is more difficult for them to carry their labor to market than for men. "While women have thus far more occasion relatively than men to move to their market, we find them disabled therefrom in a great measure by physical weakness, by timidity, and by those liabilities to misconstruction, insult, and outrage which arise out of sexual characteristics. Having more need than men to move from place to place, they have less ability to do so. It must be remembered that it is not a question merely of taking a journey from home to a place where a 'situation' has already been engaged; but it may be of seeking out employment from street to street and from shop to shop, by repeated inquiries, often through much urgency, and persistency of application."[1]

One other reason why women's wages are lower than men's is that the former seldom learn trades, or fit themselves for permanent callings. For the most part, they are looking to an early termination of any pursuit which may be adopted. This is itself a partial disqualification for any vocation.

The principal remedy for the disadvantage to which women are thus subject is, as I conceive, the removal of restrictions which custom and a wrong public sentiment have established in respect to their occupations. That this is already constantly taking place, no one can doubt; and the natural results are obvious. Within the last thirty years the wages of women have advanced very much more than those of men.

[1] F. A. Walker: The Wages Question, p. 376.

CHAPTER VIII.

PROFITS.

1. The term *profits* has already been defined as the portion of the joint product of labor and capital which goes to the *employer*. It is sometimes loosely spoken of as the *capitalist's* share. This is incorrect. The loaners of money, or of real estate, or of other property, are capitalists; and what they receive for these comes under the heads of *interest* and *rent*.

The employer may be and often is a capitalist, but he is not always and necessarily so. The distinction between the two has already been noted. "Capital cannot move itself. Labor cannot command capital, and therefore has little power; hence the necessity for an employer or *business-man* to effect a union, and put both in successful operation. Capital without labor is an infant: labor without capital is a cripple."[1]

2. The ability to organize and manage a business, and the skill involved therein, especially if there be much capital and many laborers, entitle the possessor to a larger share of the product than an ordinary laborer can command. The very principle which is the basis of distribution, and from which the law governing it is evolved, is that each producer is entitled to an equivalent of the value by him created. If one man

[1] Amasa Walker: The Science of Wealth, p. 311.

can catch twice as many fish as another, or if one boy picks three quarts of berries while another picks only one, evidently each is entitled to all he secures, and no more. The girl who tends six looms ought to have larger compensation than the one who tends but two. So, if one man brings to a business a certain high order of talent, and by its exercise so organizes and manages the labor and the capital that ten or twenty times as much is produced as would be without such directions, then a larger share of the result properly belongs to him than to an ordinary workman. Few men would put forth exertion simply for the public good, especially when it is morally certain that many would take advantage of such action to escape toil, and live upon the product of the better disposed. This would especially be the case with those competent to be employers. The responsibilities and cares of business would not be assumed by a man who knew that in so doing, though he might be the cause of manifold greater production, he would only secure for himself the same compensation as an irresponsible laborer. He would suffer far less by declining, than the rest of the community; since it depends largely upon the competent employer whether there shall be plenty of work at good wages, or the opposite. That the most competent employers should secure large profits, does not imply a diminution, but always an increase, of wages.

3. Another element which enters into the calculation of the just claims of profits is, the *risk and uncertainty* attaching to a business enterprise. Disasters are liable to occur in every undertaking. The most careful foresight cannot anticipate some of these. The profits of a business, whatever their rate, will be in no two successive years the same. Sometimes there will be positive loss. Hence allowance must be made, not only for making up actual losses, but for

the years in which the gains fall below the normal rate. A part of the losses can be calculated with approximate correctness. There will be a certain number of fires, of shipwrecks, and of other disasters, within a certain period of time, and in a given number of enterprises. Insurance companies base their calculations upon such data. The insurance premiums themselves are a part of the expense of the business, and must be deducted before the proportion of profits can be determined. But there are other liabilities which are quite incalculable, — the failure of crops, and disasters in mining operations, diminishing the material to be worked up; financial revulsions, affecting trade and decreasing consumption; and a thousand other incidents and influences.

We have seen that the doctrine largely prevailing concerning wages is, that they are paid by capital. In estimating profits on this hypothesis, we should naturally deduct from the gross profit what had been paid out for wages, to replace capital so expended. Then, after subtracting all expenditures for repairs, wear and tear of machinery, insurance, interest, losses, etc., the remainder would be profits. There is a doctrine growing out of the above, and going in general with that of the wages-fund, that profits are inversely as wages. Yet, if the conclusions at which we have arrived on several points are true, this is not so. It is, rather, as Professor Walker teaches, that profits are in no case, nor in any part, taken from wages. The probable truth of the matter is, that the larger either is, — other things being equal, — the larger will be the other.

4. It has been stated, that in this country we have, strictly speaking, no *monopolies*. We find something like an exception to this in the case of *patent* and *copy rights*. These are held to be both just and economical. It has been urged

against this view, that such privileges are of no real advantage to the community; that a benevolent man will delight to confer upon society every such boon of which he has been the creator; that the honor and fame of the invention are a sufficient inducement to the exercise of the ability implied; that many of these inventions are accidental, and cost the inventor nothing; that, in many instances, devices are sought as an aid in the particular work of the originator, and that the advantage thus gained is a sufficient incentive. Hence it is inferred that the only economical reason for exclusive privilege is removed, since there would be as many useful inventions without as with it.

But, on the other hand, it must be evident that a majority of the inventions which aid in the multiplication of wealth involve sacrifices which would never be incurred but for the hope of reward; and that, even in the case of those who are mainly moved to their undertaking by public spirit, this hope adds a stimulus without which, in many instances, the enterprise would fail. Sometimes a man has spent a large fortune, and given many years to the devising of plans and instruments, by which humanity will be benefited for ages to come. To such a man, no compensation likely to be bestowed will be more than a small fraction of the good conferred.

The case of the author is similar to that of the inventor. If, by diligence and self-denial, combined with a certain ability, he has produced a book of value, he is entitled to remuneration for his labor. But, if there be no positive restriction, any one may copy the thoughts of the author, and dispose of them as his own. This appropriation of the immaterial productions of others is prevented by the provision known as the *copyright* law.

CHAPTER IX.

INTEREST.

1. INTEREST is the compensation paid for the use of capital in the form of money. Strictly speaking, when capital in any other form is loaned, the compensation for its use is reckoned as *rent*. But sometimes the loan is of other property, though regarded as money; and so the compensation is reckoned as *interest*. For instance, a man buys a farm for three thousand dollars. He is able to pay but one thousand down. He may do one of two things: he may borrow two thousand dollars, giving, as security, a mortgage on the farm, and with this and the thousand dollars of his own make the purchase; or he may pay the thousand dollars, and for the rest give the former owner a note secured by mortgage. Here he does not literally borrow the two thousand dollars; but he borrows two-thirds of the farm, with the privilege of paying for it at some future time. But the whole arrangement is as if the buyer had borrowed the two thousand dollars; that is, the unpaid-for portion of the farm is put in the form of money, and the compensation for the use is reckoned not as rent, but as interest.

2. The *rate of interest* depends on several considerations; and it differs in different countries, as well as at different times in the same country. Some of the causes determining this variation will here be set forth.

1. The rate of interest is influenced by the amount of money in circulation. Not that the rate is always inversely as the amount. Some have denied that the amount has any thing to do with the rate : others have asserted that the rate is highest when the circulation is the largest. The latter is true in some instances, but there would be little difficulty in showing that this is due to other causes than the abundance of money. Money is like other things : in general it can be bought and sold and borrowed more cheaply when it is abundant than when it is scarce. It is sometimes the case, that scarcity of money has deranged business, paralyzed industry, and produced general distrust. At such a time, there is a small demand for money, no one daring to venture upon any new business or the revival of an old one. Under such conditions, though a really small amount of money is in circulation, the amount relative to the demand is large, and interest is low.

2. It depends upon the profits of business ; and this again depends upon the industrial system and the condition of the community. If there are but few occupations, and the range of industries is limited, the rate of profits is likely to be high, and that of wages low. In the infancy of society, as we have seen, the capitalist absorbs both a very large proportion and a very large quantity of the joint product of labor and capital. But as society advances, and industry becomes diversified and labor more productive, the laborer receives both a larger quantity and a larger proportion of the product ; while the capitalist gets a smaller proportion, but a larger quantity. In accordance with this law, the rate of interest diminishes with the advance of society. The high rate of interest in some parts of the United States is owing to the scarcity of capital, the comparatively small variety of industries, the extraordinary productiveness of labor, and

the high rate of profits. The last two are closely connected. Land is abundant, cheap, fertile, and easily cultivated. Hence a little money invested in agriculture gives good returns. Labor as well as money is scarce : the product of the laborer, in proportion to his wages, is greater than almost anywhere else. In all the industries, not only is the *rate* of wages and of profits higher, but the *aggregate* of profits is larger. As it is this which determines the prosperity of the community, the people are generally in better condition than in other countries, in spite of the high rate of interest. Yet we see, that just in proportion as industry becomes varied, and commerce increases, in any section of the country, the rate of interest diminishes.

3. The rate of interest is affected by both the scarcity and the uncertainty of capital. (*a*) If the people are vicious, indolent, and reckless of their obligations, it will be unsafe to invest property in such a community; and capitalists will not do it except at a high rate of interest. (*b*) The character of the government will have much influence. If it is weak and inefficient; if the laws are inadequate, and feebly executed ; if contracts are not enforced, and crime is unpunished, — capitalists will not loan, except on usurious conditions. If the government is of the opposite character, other things being equal, the rate is likely to be low. (*c*) The general thrift of the community has something to do with the security of capital. It is safer in a community where men are enterprising and public-spirited, where there is frugality and economy, than in one of an opposite character. A declining community, where property is constantly depreciating, is not a good one in which to invest capital.

4. Finally, the rate of interest depends on the facility with which the evidences of debt can be re-converted into money. It is frequently the case, that persons have money which

they would be glad to loan temporarily, even at a low rate : but they are liable to need it at any time ; and they must either keep it on hand, or so loan it that they can claim it again at the shortest notice. Borrowers will not be willing to pay as much for the use of money for the return of which they may be suddenly called upon, as for that which may be retained for a definite and stipulated time. To many loaners of money, it is also of the greatest importance that the interest be paid regularly and punctually. They would rather have a lower rate, and have an assurance in this respect, than to be subject to uncertainty with a higher rate.

It is partly on account of the complete security, ready conversion, and prompt payment of interest, that the bonds of stable governments are considered the best investments. It is largely for this reason, that the rate of interest on these is lower than on other securities. They are always in the market, and can be bought with little difficulty by any one who wishes to invest in them. They are as readily sold whenever the holder needs the money for any other purpose.

CHAPTER X.

RENT.

1. Rent, or the portion of the product going to the owner of any land on which any industry depends, has always been a subject of leading importance in political economy. Yet what is strictly signified by rent is of less consequence here in the United States than in most other countries. Here, to a greater extent than elsewhere, the owner and the occupier of land are the same person. The agricultural interest among us is supported mainly by men who own farms of moderate size; and, though in some parts of the country there are those who severally hold estates of thousands of acres, still the owners are usually also the managers of the whole business of their plantations. In many parts of the Continent of Europe, and more largely still in Asia, the occupants of the soil are not the owners. The proprietor leases the land to certain parties, who convey to him a stipulated proportion of the product. Sometimes this is paid in kind, but frequently there is a commutation in money.

It might seem more in accordance with the condition of things in our own land, to have discussed this subject in another connection. Still, as rent is closely connected with the occupancy and value of land, and as these subjects have been so largely discussed under this title, and there are so many both errors and valuable doctrines that have been evolved under this method of treatment, we shall probably get a better view of the phenomena in this way than in any other.

2. Land is altogether the most important instrument and condition of wealth which is furnished to man. Out of it originally come all the materials upon which the labor of man can confer value. Though it is not independent of extraneous conditions, and though its products would be of small account without the co-operation of other agencies, yet other things are more dependent upon it than it upon any of them.

It is furnished by nature, like air and water and sunshine; but, unlike them for the most part, it can be appropriated. It can also be cultivated as they cannot It may not merely be made to produce something, but its capabilities may be indefinitely increased. It is also capable of deterioration. Like other instruments, it may be worn out and spoiled.

3. What constitutes value in land? J S. Mill and others hold that it has what is called a "monopoly value," and that this makes an essential difference between it and other property. Commodities have a value bearing some sort of relation to the amount of labor requisite to their reproduction. But land, it is said, cannot be produced by labor; hence its original value is not determinable by this standard. Nor is it valued merely according to the improvements made on it. When a man purchases a piece of land, he is supposed to calculate the amount of profit he can make from it by employing his own labor or that of others upon it. The reason for the peculiarities in the character of land is represented to be, that certain individuals, having acquired a command or control of the land in a country, intercept the bounty of nature, and exact a price for that which was de-

signed to be freely bestowed. This comes, according to
Mr. Mill, from "the limitation of its quantity."

Mr. Carey, on the other hand, teaches that land is under
the same law as that which affects the value of all other
commodities; that whatever value it has, has been created
by labor, and is to be estimated, as in the case of other valuables, by the amount of labor which would be necessary to
bring it to its present condition could it be again taken in
its primitive estate. Land itself, in its natural relations, has
no value. It is that which is done on it, or in some relation
to it, which gives it value.

4. *Ricardo's theory of rent* has been accepted by a large
and reputable class of economists, both in Great Britain and
the United States, for the last fifty or sixty years. It is here
presented in the words of the author.

"On the first settling of a country in which there is an
abundance of rich and fertile land, a very small portion of
which is required to be cultivated for the support of the actual population, or indeed can be cultivated with the capital
which the population can command, there will be no rent;
for no one would pay for the use of land when there was an
abundant quantity not yet appropriated, and therefore at the
disposal of whomsoever might choose to cultivate it. . . . If
all land had the same properties, and if it were boundless in
quantity and uniform in quality, no charge would be made
for its use unless where it possessed peculiar advantages of
situation. It is only, then, because land is not unlimited in
quantity and uniform in quality, and because, in the progress
of population, land of an inferior quality or less advantageously situated is called into cultivation, that rent is ever
paid for the use of it. When, in the progress of society, land
of the second degree of fertility is taken into cultivation,
rent immediately commences on that of the first quality;

and the amount of that rent will depend on the difference in the quality of the two portions of land. . . . When land of the third quality is taken into cultivation, rent immediately commences on the second ; and it is regulated, as before, by the difference in their productive power. At the same time the rent of the first quality will rise; for that must always be above the rent of the second by the difference between the produce which they yield with a given quantity of capital and labor. With every step in the progress of population which obliges a country to have recourse to land of a worse quality, to enable it to raise its supply of food, rent on the more fertile land will rise.

" Thus, suppose land Nos. 1, 2, 3, to yield, with an equal employment of capital and labor, a net produce of a hundred, ninety, and eighty quarters of corn. In a new country, where there is an abundance of fertile land compared with the population, and where, therefore, it is only necessary to cultivate No. 1, the whole net produce will belong to the cultivator, and will be the profits of the stock which he advances. As soon as the population had so far increased as to make it necessary to cultivate No. 2, from which ninety quarters only can be obtained after supporting the laborers, rent would commence on No. 1 : for either there must be two rates of profit for agricultural capital, or ten quarters must be withdrawn from the produce of No. 1, for some other purpose. Whether the proprietor of the land or some other person cultivates No. 1, these ten quarters would equally constitute rent . for the cultivator of No. 2 would get the same result from his capital, whether he cultivated No. 1 paying ten quarters for rent, or continued to cultivate No. 2 paying no rent. In the same manner it might be shown, that, when No. 3 is brought into cultivation, the rent of No. 2 must be ten quarters or the value of ten quarters, whilst the rent of No. 1 would rise to twenty quarters; for the cultivator of No. 3 would have the same profit, whether he paid twenty quarters for the rent of No. 1, ten quarters for the rent of No. 2, or cultivated No. 3 free of rent."

5. If this doctrine be true, then there must follow from it certain very important consequences. Prominent among these would be that of the increasing ratio of rent to labor. As population increases, it is compelled to occupy always the inferior soils, so long as they can be found of sufficient fertility to yield a bare subsistence to the cultivator. It must thus follow that rent, or the proportion of the product going to the owner of the land, is always increasing; while that of the laborer is always diminishing as population increases. This, of course, is diametrically opposed to the doctrine heretofore developed, that, in an advancing community, labor is always receiving in increasing proportion of the joint product of labor and capital.

6. It is said that the increase of wealth, and the improvements in the methods and instruments of production, retard the operation of the law. But this improvement, which is implied in the progress of civilization, is but a part of the general law. It is in the very nature of things, that up to a certain limit, as men increase in number, there is a more than proportional increase in their power over nature.[1] By combination, a dozen men can often produce more than a hundred working separately. Association also tends to put each individual in possession of many of the advantages acquired by all the others. It increases the possibilities, the efficiency, and the scope of education. All these results of increase of numbers cause multiplied discoveries of new forces of na-

---

[1] Analogy would teach us, that it is a part of the more general law, that, as this limit is approached, the increase of population diminishes, and, when it is reached, the increase ceases.

ture, and lead to their manifold application in the industries, till production is enhanced incalculably.

7. If the Ricardo theory be correct, we ought to find each generation of laborers worse fed, housed, and clad than their predecessors. Mr. E. P. Smith[1] gives in tabulated form an illustration of the operation of the supposed law. We have space only for results. But suppose a moderately populated territory, with a given amount of produce, and allowing a certain natural and uniform rate of increase of population : it would be found at the end of a specified time, say two hundred years, that the " population would have multiplied two hundred and fifty-six times, food but eighty times; so that, upon equal partition, each person would obtain a little less than one-third as much food as his ancestors enjoyed two centuries before. The community, to procure the same average quantity of food as its progenitors, would require three times as much land in proportion to its numbers, and thus, in the same degree, be dispersed over greater spaces, and placed at greater distances from each other."

That the facts concerning population and sustenance are altogether the reverse of this, has been illustrated in two or three different ways. The population of every civilized nation has greatly increased within the last five hundred years. The number of the tillers of the soil has also increased. But in neither case has the increase been so great as that of the produce. The following figures from the tables of M. De Jonnes of the statistical bureau of France, tell the same story that is repeated in so many other ways : —

[1] Manual of Political Economy, pp. 54-56.

	Total Population.	Agricultural Population.	Paid to Agricultural Laborers.	Total Product.	Balance for Remainder of Population.
			Francs.	Francs.	Francs.
1700	19,500,000	15,000,000	458,000,000	1,308,000,000	859,000,000
1840	36,000,000	27,000,000	3,016,000,000	5,025,000,000	2,000,000,000

It will be seen, that, though between the two dates given the population had not doubled, the produce had nearly quadrupled; and, though the agricultural population had increased less than a hundred per cent, they had six times as much as before, while the remainder of the population had a little more than twice as much.[1]

8. The grand fallacy in this theory, as claimed by Mr. Carey, lies in the assumption that men select at first, for agricultural purposes, the richest and most productive land. This assumption is not unnatural; and yet, as matter of fact, it appears to be incorrect. It is doubtless true that a person of ordinary judgment, having reference only to immediate returns, and having the choice of two tracts of land equally advantageous in situation, but of which, with the same outlay, one would yield twenty bushels to the acre, and the other only ten, would choose the former. Other things being equal, men would select for cultivation those lands which would yield the largest returns to a given amount of labor. Yet Mr. Carey has shown, by examples from almost every part of the habitable world, that the most productive lands are very seldom those first selected for cultivation. The range of instances is so extensive, and the variety of circumstances so great, while the fact is so uniform, of the non-occupation of the richer soils before an advanced stage of civilization is

[1] E. P. Smith's Manual, p. 98.

reached, and the population greatly multiplied, that the argument is of very great weight.

Nor is this at all unaccountable. There is a satisfactory and easily apprehensible reason for it. The richest and most productive soils are almost invariably those most difficult of cultivation. When a new country begins to be settled, the population is usually small and much scattered: men cannot easily combine, and their capital is scanty. They are compelled to select the thinner soils, for the reason that they are the more easily cultivated. To go into the thick forests, where the soil is rich and heavy, and the large trees are densely crowded together, would be impossible; as, before such land could be rendered productive, the people might perish with hunger. Taking up such soils as they are able to subdue with the means at their disposal, obtaining from these enough to support life and something more, they may gradually invade the heavier soils. As the number increases, they apply themselves to the still richer lands, and always with proportionally greater returns; till, capital increasing and means multiplying, they are able to enter upon and subdue the most productive portions of the territory to which they have access. But this is not a rapid process. Up to this present time, in all civilized nations some of the most productive lands are not yet occupied. The largest returns to a given amount of labor even now in England are from lands which have been brought fully under cultivation far within the present century.

9. It would seem to follow from this theory, that the value of land arises not from the fact that all additions to the population after a certain time must resort to a less productive soil, but from the same facts which constitute a condition of all other value; namely, the labor bestowed upon the commodity. It is also highly probable that the same general law is operative here as in relation to wages and interest. The laborer is always receiving both a larger proportion and a larger quantity of the joint product of labor and capital; while the capitalist, though receiving a larger quantity, gets only a smaller proportion. It is, then, obvious, that, as a real civilization is developed, the tendency is always to equality among men. This may be retarded by the application of false principles and by bad legislation. But the great economical laws remain the same, and, if not violated, will work out beneficent results.

10. Rent — or what, for our purpose, may be considered the same thing, the value of land — is influenced by several considerations.

1. The fertility of the soil is an important element. One would be willing to pay a higher price for land, that, with a given outlay, would yield the larger returns, other things being equal. But this consideration will be materially modified by those which follow.

2. The facility or difficulty of cultivation makes a second condition. If, other things being equal, a certain tract will require the labor of four men, and will produce only fifty per cent more than another, which can be carried on by two men, the latter will be the more valuable. Yet this is also subject to modification. Here is a piece of land of exceedingly rich soil, but covered with very heavy timber, or requiring drainage; in either case involving great expenditure. The dry prairie in the neighborhood needs but little labor to render it largely productive. Five times the amount of expenditure which is bestowed on the latter might not, though repeated for two years, render the former directly capable of equal returns; but afterwards, and for all time to come, it may yield three or four times as much, to the same amount of labor, as the other. It is evident that the land which is

at first capable of the less profitable returns, might be the more valuable.

3. The third consideration is that of situation. The value of land depends principally on the value of its products; and the cost of bringing the latter to market is an important element in estimating this value. Land near a city or large town may be worth two hundred dollars an acre; while precisely the same quality of land, one hundred miles distant, and with no means of transportation except by common roads, may be worth no more than five or ten dollars. There are also other modifying elements. The more ready the access to the market, the more largely can all the capabilities of the soil be utilized. In the vicinity of great cities, a large amount of marketable produce can be raised at an immense profit, which it would pay nothing to cultivate at any considerable distance. Then, too, the nearer the land is to a densely populated town, the greater the facility of fertilization. We have seen how universal is the tendency to deterioration in land in a purely agricultural region. It needs to be in such relation to a large market-town, that a large proportion of what is produced on the farm can also be consumed on it, or that the equivalent of what is produced can be returned. Sometimes the capabilities of the soil are thus increased three, five, or even ten fold.

CHAPTER XI.

TAXATION.

1. ONE of the indispensable conditions of a prosperous community is the maintenance of order and justice between the members of the body politic. There must be protection against criminally disposed persons, and against all sorts of fraud and violence. The weak and poor and ignorant must not be allowed to be put at a disadvantage in contests with the strong and rich and intelligent; and there must be some way to decide questions of law and equity. Now, order cannot be maintained by each man's undertaking to execute justice for himself. It must be done by society in its corporate capacity. But in order to this, on the principle of the division of labor, as well as on other grounds, the duty is delegated to an agency or set of agents appointed for this purpose. This agency is *the Government*, and consists of a number of men acting in a variety of capacities.

2. Now, if these functionaries are a condition of any considerable production, then, clearly, a share of the wealth created belongs to them under the law of distribution. This is to be contributed by all who share in the benefit of the agency. The aggregate constitutes what is called *the revenue of the Government*. Its apportionment among the members of the community is known under the general name of *taxation*.

The most equable method of levying the taxes is a subject upon which a vast variety of opinions exists; and, though great improvements have been made in the devices employed, they are still very imperfect, and public men are far from agreement in regard to them. .

3. It is a question of some importance, whether a man should be taxed according to the amount of his accumulations, or of his revenues. A man may have a large estate in land or other property, which, owing to various circumstances, is bringing him in very little or even no revenue. Another has no property at all, but he has a large income from his profession or occupation. If these both pay according to property, the latter will contribute nothing, while the former will be heavily taxed. If they pay according to revenue, the latter will pay largely, and the former contribute nothing. Again, there are some so situated that they will have a *perpetual* moderate income; while others have a much larger income, which, however, depends upon the continuance of health, business prosperity, or some other contingency which is wholly uncertain. If the tax is simply according to revenue, and not property, here would be an instance of great inequality.

4. Another question arises here, which is not always squarely met by writers on this subject. Does genuine economy require a *uniform system* of taxation, according to either property or income? The *theory* of taxation, generally accepted, implies the affirmative of the above question. But it is doubtful if any civilized government ever really attempts to apply it. The economical instincts of men lead them to repudiate it in practice. Unquestionably, what men desire in respect to taxation is a system which will give the needed public revenue, at the least possible expense on the whole, and with a just distribution of the burden. But it is clearly possible, that, by attempting a literal and arithmetical apportionment, many persons may be reduced to poverty, and others to pauperism; so that some who would otherwise help to bear the burden are prevented from doing so, and others are made to add to it. It is on this account that nearly all civilized nations make certain exemptions of the property of the poor from taxation, — certain articles of prime necessity about the house, certain tools used on the farm or in the trades, certain domestic animals, and other property of a similar kind. This is not done from mere benevolence, but simply as a measure of economy. It is true that these items are exempt in the case of the rich as well as of the poor man; but, obviously, the substantial advantage accrues to the latter, as it was intended to do. They comprise but a small fraction of the wealth of the former; but they are sometimes the whole, and often the chief part, of the poor man's goods. By such exemption, thousands are encouraged, and prevented from losing hope and self-respect and independence, who otherwise might become a burden to society, thus involving an expense far greater than the amount of the small tax they would pay if there were no exemption.

There is another custom, nearly universal, which is not in harmony with the principle of uniform taxation. It is that which prevails in most modern nations, of taxing such kinds of business and such products as are admitted to be pernicious in their effects on society, at a higher rate than other kinds of business and products: spirituous liquors and tobacco come into this category. The reasonableness of this policy is obvious. If the tax is so heavy as to discourage or diminish the use of these articles, no person really suffers: on the contrary, it is scarcely disputed by any candid man, that great benefits would ensue. If diminished productiveness, if pauperism and crime, come from the use of these articles, then is the community richer from any cause tending to lessen the consumption. If a larger proportional tax will do this, it will both increase the revenue and diminish the burden.

A similar discrimination is frequently made in respect to what are called luxuries. If a heavy tax should be put upon the rich man's costly clothes, jewellery, carriages, and expensive furniture, he would not greatly suffer if he should buy somewhat less of them. But if the poor man's bread and meat and the implements of his daily toil are taxed, he cannot forego the expense of them without serious damage.

There is still another discrimination which civilized nations usually make. All property devoted to the public good, and which is used for purposes tending to diminish the evils which occasion a large proportion of the expenses of the government, is exempted. Such especially are churches and schools, and charitable and benevolent institutions. This exemption, also, is prompted by a wise economy. It renders the burdens of taxation lighter instead of heavier, and ministers largely to an increase, instead of a decrease, of public wealth.

5. Taxes are divided into *direct* and *indirect*. Direct taxation is when the tax is paid by the person upon whom it is levied. In indirect taxation the tax is levied on one person, but really paid by another. Taxes upon real estate, tools, machinery, domestic animals, etc., are direct taxes. They are supposed to be paid by the owner of the property taxed. Yet even here the tax is sometimes really paid by another party than the real owner.

Indirect taxes are levied on commodities; and the amount of the tax is added to the price of the commodity, and thus paid by the consumer. For instance, under the internal revenue system adopted during the civil war, there was a stamp-tax of one cent on every bunch of matches. The consumers paid a cent more for each bunch of matches than they otherwise would. The same is true of duties under a revenue tariff. If there be a duty of ten cents a pound on coffee, though nominally paid by the importer, it is added to the price of the article, and thus finally comes from the consumer.

6. There is some difference of opinion as to the comparative merits of direct and indirect taxation. It has been claimed in favor of the latter, (1) that it is imperceptible, and thus avoids exciting dissatisfaction in the payers; (2) that it is paid by each according to consumption, and that therefore those who consume less of the taxed article pay less of the tax; and (3) that it is divided into such minute portions as to make the payment easier.

It is true that the payment of the tax on commodities is not generally realized with much distinctness. It is regarded as a part of the price of the article, and is set down in the account of expenses as such. It is also true that the payment of the tax in minute portions prevents the conception of its real amount. Still the aggregate of all the items is none the less a burden because it is distributed over much time, and it is just as actually a subtraction from the wealth of the individual.

But these very facts are among the real and grave objections to the method. Indirect taxation is easier for the government, and less obnoxious to the people. On this account the government is less likely to be frugal and economical than if the revenues disbursed came more reluctantly from more conscious contributors. Where the people are taxed directly, they know the full amount of the cost of the government to *them*. Under such circumstances, they are far more likely to scrutinize the acts of their agents, and hold them to a strict account. It would make a great difference in the conduct of public affairs if every man knew just how much of the aggregate cost he had to pay.

It is also to be said concerning this method, that it is far more likely to be unequal than direct taxation. The duties imposed, whether excises or customs, will be paid by the consumer in proportion to the amount consumed. But if they be levied upon the necessaries of life, or even its common conveniences, the poor man must pay nearly as much as the rich. It is very easily said, that each pays in proportion to his consumption, and that he may diminish his tax by diminishing his consumption. But is it fair to compel one to the alternative of abstinence from the ordinary comforts of life, or the payment of several times his proportion towards the support of the government? Is it the part of a wise economy?

A partial remedy for this inequality is found in the taxation of luxuries which the rich use, but which the poor do not. Still, if any part of the revenue, say one-half or one-quarter, is raised from articles in most common use, the poor would evidently have to pay an undue proportion of that part.

7. There are several forms of direct taxation. The following are the principal: 1. The *income-tax*. Abstractly this is the fairest and most equable of all the forms of raising a revenue. Under this method, equality of taxation, so far as that is desirable, would be more closely approximated than under any other. Still, it is not popular, and in recent times governments rarely resort to it. That a method so fair and just should be so unpopular and so little used, is singular. Probably it is partly for the same reason that indirect is preferred to direct taxation. People would rather pay their taxes without knowing it. It is also objectionable by reason of its inquisitorial character. Business-men do not like to have their affairs examined by public officers. There is much opportunity for fraud; and thus, while dishonest men escape the payment of a large proportion of what is justly due from them, men of integrity have to pay more than their share. The situation of two persons having the same income is often so different, that the tax may be far more burdensome to one than to the other. These and some other reasons render the method unpopular.

2. The second method of direct taxation is that of assessing the whole property, real and personal, according to its estimated value. This, with some exceptions soon to be noted, is, if fairly carried out, the most equable of any save that of the income-tax. It is generally according to one's ability; and, though one's revenues are not always proportional to one's property, there are often some partial compensations for this. Still, evidently there can be no absolute equality.

The exceptions referred to are as follows: First, there are the exemptions mentioned in section 4: these are recognized by all really enlightened states, and do not need to be further discussed. Secondly, all property devoted to the public use, and from which the holders receive no revenue: this principle, too, has been examined, and the reasons in its favor set forth; it appears to be a principle of sound economy on the whole, and one diminishing, instead of increasing, the burden of taxation.

There is, however, much difficulty in adjusting this method, mainly because a considerable portion of the wealth of a community exists in invisible and intangible forms, and can thus be easily concealed. Property is also liable to double taxation, as in the case of mortgages. In some of the States, the mortgagor is required to pay the tax on the whole property; while at the same time the mortgagee is taxed for the portion mortgaged. This is manifestly unjust.

But, aside from this, there are great difficulties in ascertaining all the personal property; and, unless some method can be devised for doing this, every attempt to tax all property will be nugatory. According to the best information available, it appears, that, in the State of New York, only about fifteen per cent of the actual value of the personal property is returned by the assessors, and taxed. The same is probably true in some other States.

8. For these reasons, it has been advised by eminent writers, that a system of taxation, based wholly on *expenditure*, should be substituted for all those based on *property*. This need not be calculated by any detailed or itemized estimate, but as indicated by a single item; namely, that of *rent*. It is averred, that there is no surer index of a man's pecuniary ability than that found in this item of his expenditures. In the case of those who live in houses of their own, the rent of the house is to be estimated by that of other similar residences. This would leave untaxed all personal property, except that of certain corporations whose property-value it is easy to determine.

Probably this plan, like many others, would be found greatly faulty; and it is doubtful if any system can be devised which will commend itself as very nearly equable.

AN IMPORTANT ANNOUNCEMENT.

THE CHAUTAUQUA PRESS.

IN order to create a permanent library of useful and standard books for the homes of our C. L. S. C. members, and to reduce the expense of the Seal courses, we have organized the CHAUTAUQUA PRESS.

The first issues of the Chautauqua Press will be "THE GARNET SERIES," four volumes in the general line of the "required readings" for the coming year, as follows:—

READINGS FROM RUSKIN.

With an Introduction by H. A. BEERS, Professor of English Literature in Yale College.

This volume contains chapters from Ruskin on "The Poetry of Architecture," "The Cottage — English, French, and Italian," "The Villa — Italian," and "St. Mark's," from "Stones of Venice."

READINGS FROM MACAULAY.

With an Introduction by DONALD G MITCHELL ("Ik Marvel").

This volume contains Lord Macaulay's Essays on "Dante," "Petrarch," and "Machiavelli," "Lays of Ancient Rome," and "Pompeii."

ART, AND THE FORMATION OF TASTE.

By LUCY CRANE.

With an Introduction by CHARLES G. WHITING of "The Springfield [Mass.] Republican."

This volume contains lectures on "Decorative Art, Form, Color, Dress, and Needlework," "Fine Arts," "Sculpture," "Architecture," "Painting."

THE LIFE AND WORKS OF MICHAEL ANGELO.

By R. DUPPA [BOHN'S EDITION].

With an Introduction by CHARLES G. WHITING.

Any graduate or undergraduate of the C. L. S. C. reading the four volumes of the CHAUTAUQUA LIBRARY GARNET SERIES will be entitled to the new Garnet Seal (University Seal) on his diploma.

These volumes are designed as much for the general market as for members of the C. L. S. C., and will form the nucleus of a valuable library of standard literature.

PRICE OF EACH VOLUME, 75 CENTS.
OR $3 FOR THE SET, ENCLOSED IN NEAT BOX.

Address

CHAUTAUQUA PRESS,
117 Franklin Street, Boston, Mass.

www.ingramcontent.com/pod-product-compliance
Lightning Source LLC
Chambersburg PA
CBHW031815220426
43662CB00007B/656